I believe

THE APOSTLES' CREED

by Tim Chester

I Believe
The good book guide to the Apostles' Creed

Reprinted 2009, 2010, 2012, 2014, 2015, 2016, 2019, 2021.

Published by:
The Good Book Company

thegoodbook.com | thegoodbook.co.uk
thegoodbook.com.au | thegoodbook.co.nz | thegoodbook.co.in

ISBN: 9781905564415 | Printed in India

CONTENTS

Introduction: good book guides

Every Bible-study group is different—yours may take place in a church building, in a home or in a cafe, on a train, over a leisurely mid-morning coffee or squashed into a 30-minute lunch break. Your group may include new Christians, mature Christians, non-Christians, mums and tots, students, businessmen or teens. That's why we've designed these *Good Book Guides* to be flexible for use in many different situations.

Our aim in each session is to uncover the meaning of a passage, and see how it fits into the "big picture" of the Bible. But that can never be the end. We also need to appropriately apply what we have discovered to our lives. Let's take a look at what is included:

Talkabout: Most groups need to "break the ice" at the beginning of a session, and here's the question that will do that. It's designed to get people talking around a subject that will be covered in the course of the Bible study.

Investigate: The Bible text for each session is broken up into manageable chunks, with questions that aim to help you understand what the passage is about. **The Leader's Guide** contains **guidance on questions**, and sometimes additional "follow-up" questions.

Explore more (optional): These questions will help you connect what you have learned to other parts of the Bible, so you can begin to fit it all together like a jig-saw; or occasionally look at a part of the passage that's not dealt with in detail in the main study.

Apply: As you go through a Bible study, you'll keep coming across **apply** sections. These are questions to get the group discussing what the Bible teaching means in practice for you and your church. **Getting personal** is an opportunity for you to think, plan and pray about the changes that you personally may need to make as a result of what you have learned.

Pray: We want to encourage prayer that is rooted in God's word—in line with His concerns, purposes and promises. So each session ends with an opportunity to review the truths and challenges highlighted by the Bible study, and turn them into prayers of request and thanksgiving.

The **Leader's Guide** and introduction provide historical background information, explanations of the Bible texts for each session, ideas for **optional extra** activities, and guidance on how best to help people uncover the truths of God's word.

Why study the Apostles' Creed?

Many churches recite the Apostles' Creed each week. The phrases are familiar, not only to committed Christians, but also among the wider population who grew up attending church with family or at school. Yet for many it is a dull routine, and for others it is spoken with confusion or doubt, rather than with confidence and joy.

The Apostles' Creed is one of the oldest and most widely acknowledged creeds. Tradition divides the Creed into twelve phrases—one for each of the apostles—but there is no historical evidence for this. It probably started life as a summary of Christian faith for people who wanted to be baptised. When asked: "Do you believe in God, the Father Almighty?" and so on, a Christian would reply: "I believe". This is why the Creed says "I believe", whereas most creeds say "We believe" to express the common faith of the Christian community.

As the Apostles' Creed developed, several variations existed, both in Latin and Greek, until the Creed took its final form in the eighth century. By the twelfth century it was accepted by all branches of the church as a binding statement of Christian belief. Many modern versions have "he descended to the dead" instead of "he descended into hell", including the version used in the Anglican prayer book, *Common Worship*, and this is the wording used in this course.

Do we really need creeds? Some people do not like the idea of pinning truth down. Others want to stick to the Bible alone. Certainly it is true that only the Bible is God's inspired word—creeds cannot have the same authority. But most churches have found it helpful to have a summary of Christian belief. Creeds summarise who we are, they teach us what is important, and they help us avoid error. In modern business language, they are our "identity documents". The New Testament clearly suggests there are certain truths that people deny at their peril. We should have the humility to learn from the great summaries of Christian faith put together by previous generations.

This Good Book Guide aims to fill out the content of the short statements of this Creed, packed with so much momentous truth and understanding. In these ten sessions, you will discover how the Creed's statements are derived from the Bible—the teaching of the apostles—and its life-changing significance for our daily lives. Saying the Creed need never be dull, confused or joyless again!

The Apostles' Creed

I believe in God, the Father almighty,
creator of heaven and earth.
I believe in Jesus Christ, his only Son, our Lord,
who was conceived by the Holy Spirit,
born of the Virgin Mary,
suffered under Pontius Pilate,
was crucified, died, and was buried;
he descended to the dead.
On the third day he rose again;
he ascended into heaven,
he is seated at the right hand of the Father,
and he will come again to judge
the living and the dead.
I believe in the Holy Spirit,
the holy catholic Church,
the communion of saints,
the forgiveness of sins,
the resurrection of the body,
and the life everlasting. Amen.

1 "I believe in God"

BELIEVING IN GOD

Romans 1 v 18-25; John 14 v 1-14

talkabout

1. What reasons do people give about why they don't believe in God? What do you think makes it hard for people to believe in God?

- What reasons lead you to believe that God is real?

investigate

Read Romans 1 v 18-25

In this passage from a letter written to Christians in Rome, the apostle Paul begins by explaining the mess into which the human race had fallen, which would result in God sending Jesus Christ to rescue humanity.

DICTIONARY

Wrath (v 18): deserved, justified anger.
Futile (v 21): useless, pointless.

2. According to Paul, how has God made Himself known?

3. What does Paul say we can know about God from creation?

4. According to Paul, why don't people believe in God?

apply

5. Look at verse 21. If we want to get to know God or understand Him better, where must we start?

explore more

optional

We have seen that the fundamental reason people don't believe in God is because of their hearts (their desire to enjoy wickedness instead of God), rather than their heads (responding to the evidence of God in creation) or their conscience (knowing there is right and wrong).

What are the implications for us as Christians, when we try to convince people of the truth of Christianity?

Read Deuteronomy 4 v 5-8; 1 Peter 2 v 11-12

How were God's people, in both the Old and New Testaments, to bring unbelieving people to believe in the one true God?
How might this help us convince people who suppress the truth because they will not obey God?

investigate

Read John 14 v 1-14

This passage comes from an account of Jesus' life and teaching, written by the apostle John. In these verses Jesus refers to God as "the Father". The reason why Christians turn to the words of Jesus to find out about God, rather than listening to anyone else, should become clearer as we see what Jesus had to say.

6. According to Jesus, how can we know God?

7. What does Jesus mean when He describes Himself as "the way and the truth and the life" (v 6)?

8. Jesus tells His disciples that anyone who has seen Him has seen the Father (v 9). But how can people who have not seen Jesus (like us!) know the Father? (See verse 10 and compare John 20 v 29-31.)

9. What does Jesus say about His words in verse 10?

- What does He say about the Father's work?

10. Look at **John 5 v 19-24**. What does the work of God, through the words of Jesus, actually do in this world?

11. In John 14 v 12, Jesus says that those who have faith in Him will do greater works than the miracles He did. How do Christians do the "greater works" that Jesus promises?

apply

12. What do your friends and colleagues think about how God can be known, and how He works in the world?

13. How could you use Romans 1 and John 14 to respond to these beliefs?

getting personal

If you are unsure about whether you truly know God, what have you learned in this session that can help you?

What do you need to do in the days ahead?

If you have come to know God, through listening to the words of Jesus and putting your faith in Him, to what extent are you involved in doing the "greater works" that Jesus promised?

What do you need to do in the days ahead?

pray

You may, first of all, want to pray for yourself, that you would be someone who listens to the words of Jesus, and does not suppress the truth about God. Pray also that, through Jesus, you will be someone who truly knows God and has eternal life.

Pray for your unbelieving friends by name. Ask God to give you opportunities to speak to them about the living God, who is revealed through Jesus. And ask God to bring light to their darkened hearts.

2

"I believe in God, the Father ... his only Son ... the Holy Spirit"

THE TRIUNE GOD John 17 v 20-26

talkabout

1. How would you answer the question "Who are you?" Think of a few different endings to the following sentence that will give true descriptions of yourself: *I am...*

investigate

Christians believe God has always had relationships. This is because the one God is three persons. We call this "the Trinity".

The shape of the Apostles' Creed reflects the triune God. It starts with a section on the Father, moves on to the Son and concludes with the Spirit. The Apostles' Creed began life as a statement of faith made by people who wanted to be baptised. Jesus said: "Go and make disciples of all nations, baptising them in the name of the Father and of the Son and of the Holy Spirit" (Matthew 28 v 19). So this Creed is an explanation of what it means to be baptised in the name of the Trinity.

Read John 17 v 20-26

2. What does Jesus say about His relationship with the Father?

3. How long has the Father loved the Son?

4. What does this tell us about Jesus?

5. Jesus says the Trinity is like a loving family (eg: He uses the word "Father" in v 21, 24, 25). What does He say that suggests the Trinity is more than a family of separate individuals?

Read John 15 v 26 and 16 v 12-15

6. Jesus describes the Holy Spirit as "the Advocate" or "the Helper". What does He say about the Father's relationship with the Spirit?

7. In the same verses, what does Jesus say about His own relationship with the Spirit?

Father, Son and Spirit share one being. There are not three gods. But the three persons of the Trinity also choose to define themselves in terms of their loving relationships with one another. The Father is the Father because He has a Son and so on.

apply

8. How does the triune God of the Bible differ from many commonly-held beliefs about God?

- How would you respond to someone who says that all religions lead to the same God?

optional

explore more

Read Ephesians 1 v 3-14

In these verses from Paul's letter to Christians in Ephesus, Paul describes God's eternal plan to save sinful human beings and make them His people. He focuses first on the Father (v 3-6), then on the Son (v 7-12) and finally on the Spirit (v 13-14).

What is the role of the Father in salvation?
What is the role of the Son?
And what is the role of the Spirit?

investigate

Three times in John 17 Jesus says that He was sent by the Father into the world (v 21, 23, 25). And Jesus sends the Spirit to His followers from the Father (John 15 v 26).

9. What does this tell us about the Trinity?

10. How does Jesus describe the relationship between the Trinity and Christian believers in John 17 v 20-26?

11. How will the world come to believe in God?

optional

explore more

Read Hebrews 9 v 13-14

Sinful people cannot be children of God because God is holy and just, and so He must punish sin. God's law, given to Israel in the Old Testament, required the people to make sacrifices because of their sin. These sacrifices made people outwardly clean. However, it wasn't until Jesus' death on the cross that God truly dealt with the problem of sin—past and present (Romans 3 v 25-26).

Read Romans 3 v 21-26

On the cross, who was the sacrifice and to whom was the sacrifice offered?
Who was judged and who did the judging? (See also Isaiah 53 v 4-6—an Old Testament prophecy of Jesus' death on the cross.)
God could truly deal with our sin at the cross only because He is triune. Can you explain why?

apply

We have seen that the persons of God are defined by their loving relationships with one another. We are made in the image of the triune God (see Genesis 1 v 26-27). So we find our identity through relationships—as children, husbands and wives, parents, friends and, above all, as children of God.

12. How might you use the Bible's teaching on the Trinity to advise:

- a woman who is about to leave her marriage because she wants to "find herself"?

- a student who thinks he can be a Christian without going to church?

- a young man who will not get married for fear of losing his freedom?

- a woman who feels tied down by her responsibilities to her ageing parents?

13. Jesus says the world will believe in the triune God as it sees the Christian community (v 21 and 23). When do unbelievers see the life of your Christian church or group? How can you ensure that outsiders see more of your love for one another?

getting personal

God is a "people person". Are you? What do you need to do to better reflect the love of the triune God in your relationships with others?

Which relationships in particular?

pray

Use the words of **Ephesians 1 v 3-14** to praise the glorious grace of God—Father, Son and Holy Spirit.

3 "I believe in God, the Father almighty, creator of heaven and earth"

THE SOVEREIGN GOD Psalm 33

talkabout

1. Have you ever struggled to believe that God is in control of events?

investigate

Psalm 33 speaks about how God made the world and how He continues to rule it. As the Apostles' Creed says, God the Father is "almighty" and He is the "creator of heaven and earth".

Read Psalm 33 v 1-5

2. Why should we sing joyfully to the LORD?

DICTIONARY

Upright (v 1): people who are committed to living God's way.

3. How do life's difficulties cause us to doubt what this psalm says about God in verses 4-5?

Read verses 6-9

4. How does the psalm describe God's work of creation?

5. What is the right way for us to respond to God the Creator?

Read verses 10-12

6. How is God involved in the world He has made?

DICTIONARY

Foils, thwarts (v 10): frustrates, defeats.

7. What is the focus of God's plan for history (v 12)?

apply

8. Think over what we have learned so far about God from Psalm 33. How do people often get God wrong?

• What do we need to make clear about God as we speak to others? (See Acts 17 v 22-31 for an example of how the apostle Paul speaks about the one Creator God to a multi-faith society.)

getting personal

What impression of God might people around you get from the way you live and speak about Him? Would they see your confidence in His almighty power, His unfailing love and His unshakeable purposes?

What will help you to know God better and to speak about Him?

investigate

Read verses 13-22

DICTIONARY

Deliverance (v 17): rescue.

Fear (v 18): recognise and respect.

9. What do verses 13-15 say about God's relationship to the world?

10. What do verses 16-17 say about humanity?

11. The Creator God is all-powerful and all-seeing. What does this mean for those who do not trust Him?

• What does this mean for His people?

12. How does this psalm invite us to respond to the truth that God is the almighty Creator of heaven and earth?

explore more

optional

Read Matthew 6 v 25-34

How does Jesus describe God's relationship with His people?

What does this relationship mean for Christians? Look at the following passages to find out: Matthew 5 v 43-48; 6 v 5-8; 6 v 9-15; 7 v 7-12.

apply

13. If Psalm 33 is true, why does God allow bad things to happen to His children? (See also Romans 8 v 28-30 and John 9 v 1-3.)

14. What should we remind one another of when we face difficulties in life?

getting personal

Think of the difficulties that you have faced in your life. Have you been able to keep trusting that God is both almighty in His power and unfailing in His love? What can you do now that will help you to continue trusting in your heavenly Father, whatever comes your way?

pray

Pray for yourself—that you would know God as He has revealed Himself, that you would trust Him, and that you would proclaim Him, faithfully and accurately, to others.

Pray for others—people you knowing facing difficulties, and Christian brothers and sisters persecuted for their faith. Use verse 22 as your prayer. Pray that they might hope in God and that His unfailing love will rest upon them.

"I believe in Jesus Christ, his only Son, our Lord, who was conceived by the Holy Spirit, born of the virgin Mary"

4 THE IDENTITY OF JESUS CHRIST

Hebrews 1 – 2

talkabout

1. What does our culture think about Jesus?

investigate

Read Hebrews 1 v 1-3

2. What does the writer say about Jesus? And about the relationship of Jesus to God the Father?

DICTIONARY

Prophets (v 1): messengers from God.
Sustaining (v 3): keeping going.
Purification (v 3): cleansing.

explore more

optional

Read Hebrews 1 v 4-14

What does the writer say about the relationship of Jesus to the angels?

Read Hebrews 2 v 1-4

According to Jewish tradition, the Law of Moses was given by angels. What does the writer say about the law? What does the writer say about the message of Jesus?

According to Hebrews 2 v 1, what do these truths about the identity of Jesus Christ mean for believers?
How can we drift away from the truth?
What is the result of drifting away?
How can we stop ourselves drifting away?

investigate

Read Hebrews 2 v 5-9

DICTIONARY

Subject to (v 8): ruled by.

3. In verses 6-8 the writer quotes from Psalm 8. According to the quotation, what was God's intention for humanity?

4. What is the reality of human rule over God's world?

5. How will humanity's role in God's creation be restored?

Humanity was to rule over and care for God's creation on God's behalf. But, because of our disobedience, our rule over the world became corrupt and limited. Jesus entered our humanity to restore humanity's reign over the world. He is like a new Adam (Adam = the first man).

Jesus shows us what it is to be truly human.

apply

6. How should this truth—that humanity's rule will be restored in Jesus—affect our attitude to the environment?

7. "We see Jesus ... now crowned with glory and honour" (v 9). This is not how the rest of the world sees Him yet. How do we "see" Jesus like this?

getting personal

Do you "see" Jesus now crowned with glory and honour? And have you grasped the big picture of what He came to do? Do you look forward to the day when He will be seen by everyone to be crowned with glory and honour, as He comes to restore creation and His people to the glory and perfection that God first gave?

How can you live today in the light of this wonderful hope?

investigate

Read verses 10-18

8. What does the writer mean when he says God made Jesus perfect (= qualified) through what he suffered (v 10)?

DICTIONARY

High priest (v 17): in the Old Testament, the high priest made a sacrifice which allowed the people to be forgiven.
Make atonement for (v 17): deal with something that makes people enemies, so that they become friends.

Jesus always was and is fully God. He is God's only eternal Son, the heir of all things, Maker of the universe and the exact representation of the Father's being (Hebrews 1 v 2-3). But Jesus also became fully human and experienced human suffering. We call this the "incarnation" = God becoming human. Jesus became the human representative of His people. We are His family and He is our brother.

9. According to verses 14-15, why did Jesus become human?

10. How does Jesus set us free?

11. Write a summary of why Jesus became human, according to Hebrews 2. (Use your answers to questions in this session to help you.)

optional

explore more

Read Matthew 1 v 18-25

The Apostles' Creed says Jesus "was conceived by the Holy Spirit" and "born of the Virgin Mary". The writers of the Creed believed that it was important that Christians affirm the virgin birth.

What reasons do people give for not believing in the virgin birth? What do these reasons reveal about the people who put them forward?

Compare **Isaiah 7 v 14** with **Matthew 1 v 23**. *Why is it important that Christians believe that the virgin birth was a true historical event?*

What important truth about God's involvement in His plan of salvation does the virgin birth demonstrate?

apply

12. When we struggle with sin, how does it help to know that Jesus was fully human?

- What should we do then, when we are being tempted (see Hebrews 4 v 14-16)?

getting personal

You may have always viewed Jesus as someone remote—too holy and exalted for you to approach directly in prayer. How does this session change that view, and your relationship with Jesus?

If you understand that Jesus knows what it is like to be tempted and to suffer, does that make a difference to what you do when you are faced with similar circumstances?

pray

Think about what you have learned in this session and come up with one thing that you need to…
- praise God for
- thank God for
- say sorry to God for

Use the words of Hebrews 4 v 14-16 to pray for mercy and grace to help Christians you know in their time of need.

"I believe in Jesus Christ ... who ... suffered under Pontius Pilate, was crucified, died and was buried; he descended to the dead"

5 THE SACRIFICE OF JESUS CHRIST

Matthew 27 v 11-54

talkabout

1. At the heart of Christianity is a brutal execution. How would you explain the death of Jesus, and why it is so central to the Christian faith?

investigate

Read Matthew 27 v 11-26

2. What did Pilate make of Jesus?

DICTIONARY

Governor (v 11): ie: Pontius Pilate, the Roman governor who ruled Jerusalem and the surrounding area.

Festival (v 15): the Jewish Passover festival.

3. Who was guilty and who was innocent? Who was condemned and who went free?

4. What does Matthew's account of the choice between Jesus and Barabbas show us about the significance of the cross?

Matthew tells the story of the trial of Jesus to give us a picture of what happened at the cross. Jesus the innocent One was judged so that the guilty—including us if we have faith in Jesus—can go free.

Read verses 27-44

DICTIONARY

Gall (v 34): a bitter-tasting plant.
Casting lots (v 35): playing a game of chance.

5. What did the Romans make of the claim that Jesus is God's King?

• What do you think they expected from a king?

6. What did the Jews make of the claim that Jesus is God's Saviour?

• What do you think they expected from a saviour?

7. What did the Jews make of the claim that Jesus is God's Son?

• What do you think they expected from someone who claimed to be the Son of God?

apply

8. Jesus did not match people's expectations of a king or saviour. What kind of a King and Saviour is He, then?

• How can Christians still have wrong expectations of Jesus?

getting personal

If you are a Christian, how much does your life reflect the King that you follow? Do you live to get honour, power or influence in this world?

Or are you giving up your own interests and comforts to help others, to spread the life-giving good news of Jesus, and to bring glory to God?

In which areas do you need to change?

investigate

Read verses 45-54

DICTIONARY

Elijah (v 47): an Old Testament prophet.

9. What is the significance of the darkness in verse 45? (Compare Psalm 105 v 26-28.)

10. So why was Jesus forsaken by God (v 46)?

explore more

optional

Some versions of the Apostles' Creed say that Jesus "descended into hell". Some Christians have thought that Jesus entered hell to break down its gates and set people free.

Read Hebrews 9 v 24-26

Where does Jesus "go" in these verses?

How does He set His people free?

What does it mean to confess that Jesus "descended into hell" or "to the dead"?

11. What is the significance of the torn curtain (v 51)? (Compare Exodus 26 v 31-35.)

12. What is the significance of the open tombs (v 52-53)?

apply

13. We do not expect God to die in shame. But the cross reveals the true God to us (v 54). What does the cross show us about the character of God?

14. What kinds of things do people think will make their prayers more effective?

- What does make our prayers effective?

getting personal

How do you view the God that you pray to? Why do you think that God listens (or doesn't listen) to your prayers? What have you learned that can give you confidence to approach God in prayer?

pray

Use the hymn "When I survey the wondrous cross" by Isaac Watts as the basis for your prayers.

When I survey the wondrous cross
on which the Prince of glory died,
my richest gain I count but loss,
and pour contempt on all my pride.

Forbid it, Lord, that I should boast,
save in the death of Christ my God;
all the vain things that charm me most,
I sacrifice them to His blood.

See from His head, His hands, His feet,
sorrow and love flow mingled down;
did e'er such love and sorrow meet,
or thorns compose so rich a crown?

Were the whole realm of nature mine,
that were an offering far too small;
love so amazing, so divine,
demands my soul, my life, my all!

"On the third day he rose again; he ascended into heaven, he is seated at the right hand of the Father, and he will come again to judge the living and the dead"

6 THE REIGN OF JESUS CHRIST

1 Corinthians 15 v 1-34

talkabout

1. Share your experiences of events that took over your whole life as you were preparing for them.

investigate

The Apostles' Creed says that Jesus "rose again" and that He "will come again". The resurrection of Jesus means that death is not the end for Christians. Rather, our resurrection at the return of Christ should dominate our lives in the present, as we will see in the following passage from Paul's first letter to the church in Corinth.

Read 1 Corinthians 15 v 1-11

2. Verses 1-8 are a summary of the gospel—the Christian message. Why does Paul say the gospel is the most important news in the world (v 1-3)?

DICTIONARY

In vain (v 2): for nothing.
Apostles (v 7): men handpicked by the risen Jesus to build His church and write the New Testament.
Abnormally born (v 8): the other apostles knew Jesus during His time on earth, but He appeared to Paul after He ascended to heaven (see Acts 9).

3. What is the message of the gospel?

4. What does Paul say about the death of Jesus?

5. How does Paul emphasise the reality of Christ's resurrection?

6. Why does Paul emphasise the resurrection in his gospel summary (v 12)?

Read verses 12-19

7. What would things be like if Christ had not risen from the dead?

DICTIONARY

Testified (v 15): claimed.
Futile (v 17): useless.
Fallen asleep (v 18): died.

apply

8. There are many opinions today about what happens after death. How is the Christian answer to that question more credible and more thrilling than any alternative?

- How should the truth of the resurrection affect our attitude to the difficulties we all face: sickness, ageing, disappointment, failure, etc?

getting personal

How often do you thank God for your future resurrection? Do you look forward to the future with joy or fear?

Have you ever used the hope of resurrection to comfort yourself or a fellow Christian facing a time of difficulty?

If the truth of the resurrection doesn't thrill you, why is that and what do you need to do about it?

investigate

Read verses 20-28

9. In what way are Adam and Christ similar?

DICTIONARY

Firstfruits (v 20): in the Old Testament, these were the first portion of the grain Israel harvested, which showed that God was giving a full harvest. Paul uses it here as a term meaning "preview" or "first instalment".

Dominion (v 24): rule.

10. What are the differences between Adam and Christ?

11. The Apostles' Creed says that Jesus "ascended into heaven" and "is seated at the right hand of the Father". What is the significance of this?

optional

explore more

The Creed says that Jesus "will come again to judge the living and the dead" (the phrase is taken from 2 Timothy 4 v 1). Verse 25 says: "He must reign until he has put all his enemies under his feet".

Read John 5 v 19-30

Who will judge humanity? On what basis will people be judged? When will judgment take place?

Imagine someone cuts in front of you while you are driving your car. How do you respond? How should this truth change our natural response?

Read Romans 12 v 14-21

How should we respond when we are wronged? What does our impatience for judgment reveal about us? How can we avoid being judgmental?

apply

Read verses 29-34

12. If Christ has not been raised and we will not be raised, what would be the logical way to live?

- Since there is a resurrection, what is the logical way to live?

13. In verse 10, Paul says God's grace in his life was not "in vain" (ESV). In verse 58, he uses the same phrase again when he says our labour is not "in vain". It means "empty" or "pointless". The resurrection gives our lives meaning and purpose. What is that purpose (v 10-11, 58)?

getting personal

What would people assume you believed about life after death if they looked at your lifestyle? Has anyone ever commented on or asked you about your hope of resurrection (1 Peter 3 v 15)?

Does your life have the same purpose as Paul's? How has this session encouraged you to give yourself more fully to the work of the Lord?

pray

Read Matthew 6 v 19-21. Before offering prayers of thanksgiving and request, reflect in silence on whether you are living for this life or for the life to come.

7 "I believe in the Holy Spirit"
THE LIFE OF THE SPIRIT

Romans 8 v 1-17

⊖ talkabout

1. How do people today answer the question: What's wrong with the world? Share some commonly suggested answers and discuss how near or far from the truth they are.

⊻ investigate

There are many things wrong with the world, but the Bible says they have one common source: human hearts that are trapped in sin. In Romans 8, Paul explains how the Holy Spirit sets us free from sin and its consequences, to live as God's children.

Read Romans 8 v 1-4

2. What was God's law powerless to do?

Verse	What is done for the Christian	How / Why?	What the law couldn't do
v 1-2			
v 3			
v 4			

• What must be done about past sin (v 3)?

3. The "law of sin and death" is the principle that sin and death dominate the existence and destinies of every human born into this world. How have believers been set free from the law of sin and death?

• What part does the Spirit play?

There is no condemnation for Christians (v 1) because God has already condemned our sin through the sacrificial death of own Son (v 3). Jesus set us free from the power of sin (= slavery) and the penalty of sin (= death). The work of Christ in the past on the cross is applied to our lives in the present by the Spirit. That is why Paul calls the gospel "the law of the Spirit who gives life" (v 2). Paul says the Spirit is "the Spirit of God" and "the Spirit of Christ" (v 9). The Spirit is God living in us (v 10-11).

Read verses 5-11

4. What are people like who are controlled by their "flesh" (or "sinful natures", NIV84) (v 5-8)?

5. What happens when we become Christians, according to verse 9?

6. How is the life of the Spirit different from the slavery of the flesh? Look again at verses 5-8 and contrast the two types of people.

7. Look at verses 10-11. Why does Paul call the Spirit "the Spirit who gives life" in verse 2?

Read verses 12-14

DICTIONARY

Obligation (v 12): duty.

When we become Christians, we receive the Spirit to help us please God. But our sinful nature, our "flesh", has not gone away yet. The result is a struggle between the life of the Spirit and the habits of our old way of life.

8. What is Paul's warning in verses 12-14?

apply

9. What does it mean for us to "put to death the misdeeds of the body" (v 13)?

- What does the image of "putting to death" tell us about the Christian's struggle against sin?

- What might this look like in everyday life?

10. From these verses, how could you encourage and challenge someone who says: "I can't help sinning"?

getting personal

If someone looked at your life, would they see that you are involved in a struggle against sin? If you have become complacent, what do you need to do? If you are discouraged and at the point of giving up, what will help you to keep struggling?

investigate

Read verses 14-17

11. What does Paul say the Spirit does for Christians in verses 14-17?

12. Look again at verses 14-17. What does it mean to be children of God?

optional

explore more

In verses 14-17, Paul's words reflect the story of how God's people got from Egypt to the promised land. This Old Testament story was a picture of what God would do through His Son and His Spirit. This story has become our story. *What are the links?*

13. Summarise what verses 1-17 say about the role of the Holy Spirit in the life of the believer.

apply

14. Imagine someone who doubts they are a Christian because they continue to sin. What would you say to them?

getting personal

How certain are you that you are a forgiven child of God? Is there a particular struggle with sin in your life that is making you doubt whether you can call God "Father"? What is your relationship with God based on—how good you have been, or what Jesus has done for you?

pray

Use the language of Romans 8 v 1-17 to praise God for the amazing privilege of becoming His children and being able to call Him our Father.

"I believe in ... the holy catholic Church, the communion of saints"

8 THE COMMUNITY OF THE SPIRIT

Ephesians 1 – 4

talkabout

1. "Jesus is okay; it's the church I can't stand." Why do people say things like this? How do you react to these kinds of statements?

investigate

Read Ephesians 1 v 1-8

DICTIONARY

Redemption (v 7): to be set free.

2. What does Paul these Christians (v 1). What is he telling them about the Christian life?

"Holy people" is also translated "saints" (NIV84). The Apostles' Creed talks of "the communion of saints". "Communion" here does not mean the Lord's Supper or the Eucharist. It means "community" or "fellowship". It is the same word that Paul uses in the short prayer known as the Grace (2 Corinthians 13 v 14), when he speaks of "the fellowship of the Holy Spirit".

A church is a community of Christians. The church is the family of the Father (1 v 4-5), the body of Christ (1 v 23) and the community of the Holy Spirit (2 v 22).

3. From this passage, what does it mean to say the church is a holy community? (See also Ephesians 5 v 25-27.)

Read verses 18-23

4. Summarise what God the Father has done for Christ.

DICTIONARY

Enlightened (v 18): given sight or understanding..

5. For what purpose has God done this?

apply

6. How do you generally think and feel about church on, say, Sunday mornings? And what do you think shapes your attitude?

- To what extent do these attitudes reflect (or fail to reflect) the fact that church is made up of sinners who have been graciously adopted as sons of God, to be the bride, the body and the fulness of Christ, God's chosen and supreme King?

getting personal

Have you ever truly grasped the awesome depth of God's love, and the extent of His plans for His people? How will these truths about the church affect your attitude next time you meet with your Christian brothers and sisters?

investigate

The Apostles' Creed says the church is "catholic". It is not talking about the Roman Catholic church. "Catholic" means "universal". The church includes people from every nation. No ethnic or social group is left out.

Read Ephesians 2 v 11-22

7. What was the position of the Gentiles before the time of Jesus?

8. What is the status of non-Jews now who are "in Christ Jesus"?

DICTIONARY

Gentiles (v 11): not Jews.
Uncircumcised/circumcision (v 11): God told His Old Testament people to be circumcised as a physical sign that they were His people.
Covenants (v 12): binding agreements.
Reconcile (v 16): bring into friendship.
Consequently (v 19): because of this.
Foreigners (v 19): outsiders.

9. How has Christ made the church for everyone? Look at what is said in the following verses:
   - v 12-13: What has the blood of Christ done?

   - v 16: Who has been reconciled to whom?

• v 14-15 (also v 11): What divided people previously? What has Christ now done?

• v 18: What is it that unites everyone who is in Christ?

10. When all types of people are reconciled in church, what does this show God's enemies (3 v 10-11)?

11. Look at verses 19-22. Paul describes the church (God's people, not a building) as God's temple. What does this tell us about the church?

optional

explore more

Read 1 Corinthians 12 v 12-26

Here, Paul again describes the church as the body of Christ, but in much greater detail. Discuss how you would use these verses to reply to the following statements:

"I'm going to give up going to church. I can't find anyone like me there."

"We've had a couple of newcomers at church recently, but neither of them were the sort of people we're looking for."

"I never say anything about my problems at church. Everyone there is so stable and well-adjusted. I don't know what they would think of me."

What keeps the body together?

apply

Read Ephesians 4 v 1-6

> **DICTIONARY**
>
> **Bearing with (v 2):** putting up with.

12. Since all kinds of people have been reconciled in Christ, how should Christians live, and what does that mean in practice?

- What stops Christians from living like this?

- What antidote is found in these verses?

Read verses 7-13

> **DICTIONARY**
>
> **Apportioned (v 7):** allocated/decided.

13. Who in the church is responsible for serving God and building up the church? Who is responsible for helping them?

- How should this affect what we do when we meet together with other Christians?

Read Ephesians 4 v 25 – 5 v 2

14. What principles does Paul give for how we should live as members of the Christian community? It may be helpful to complete the following table:

Verse	Right behaviour	Reason	Wrong behaviour	*How am I doing?*
4 v 25		v 25		
4 v 26		v 27		
4 v 28		v 28		
4 v 29		v 29		
4 v 30		2 v 22		
4 v 31-32		5 v 1-2		

pray

Read through Paul's prayer for the whole church in **Ephesians 3 v 16-21**. Spend time thanking God for your Christians brothers and sisters, and make Paul's prayer your own as you ask God to help you grow together as a fellowship of saints.

9 "I believe in ... the forgiveness of sins"

THE WORK OF THE SPIRIT

Matthew 9 v 1-13; Titus 3 v 3-8

talkabout

1. What does our culture think about sin?

 • And what does our culture think about forgiveness?

investigate

Read Matthew 9 v 1-13

2. Imagine what the paralysed man and his friends would have expected from Jesus, and compare Jesus' actions in verse 2. What does Jesus show us about God's priorities?

3. Look at verses 9-13. What do the actions of Jesus show us about God's forgiveness?

4. How do the words of Jesus in this passage explain His actions?

optional

explore more

In verse 13, Jesus quotes from the prophet Hosea.

Read Hosea 1 v 2-3 and 3 v 1-5

How does Gomer treat Hosea? How does Hosea treat Gomer?

What does their relationship teach us about God's relationship to His people?

apply

5. How should the actions and words of Jesus shape our view of ourselves?

- How is this different from the attitudes of our culture?

6. How should the actions and words of Jesus shape our view of those who are "outcasts" in our society?

• How is this different from the attitudes of our culture?

getting personal

Think of those who are considered "outsiders" in our society.

How do you compare yourself with them? Do you believe any difference is down to your own goodness, common-sense and self-discipline, or to the grace of God—His undeserved kindness?

If you know people who are outcasts, what can you do right now to show compassion to them?

investigate

Read Matthew 15 v 17-20

7. What is the source of our sinful actions?

8. What happens if we just try to change our actions?

• **Read Ezekiel 36 v 25-27.** What do we need?

Read Titus 3 v 3-8

DICTIONARY

Justified (v 7): made not guilty.
Grace (v 7): undeserved kindness.

9. What does Paul mean in verse 3 when he says we were "enslaved by all kinds of passions"?

10. What are some of the ways in which we are deceived by sin (v 3)?

11. In verse 3, Paul describes what we were "at one time". What has happened to Christians to change this?

12. Paul says that Christians have been washed, reborn and renewed by the Holy Spirit. How do these three things overcome the problem of sin?

- Washed (see also Matthew 15 v 18-20):

- Reborn (see also Romans 5 v 12):

- Renewed (see also Ephesians 2 v 1):

We have been "justified"—made right with God (v 7). Our past, present and future sins have all been forgiven by God. But God is also changing us. He gives us the Holy Spirit to help us live a new life, free from sin.

apply

13. Paul teaches that without the Holy Spirit, we could not change. But what does Paul expect believers to do as a result of this teaching (v 8)?

- There is a connection between the work of the Spirit in changing Christians, and the responsibility of Christians to change. In what ways do people get this wrong?

14. Paul reminds us in verse 7 that we are made right with God by His grace. But we still do wrong things. Being changed by the Holy Spirit is a process. What happens if we forget it is a process?

getting personal

How might you have misunderstood the work of the Spirit in your life?

Do you expect to be made perfect in this life, rather than the life to come?

Have you become complacent about devoting yourself to doing good, expecting the Spirit to do all the hard work for you?

Which is the biggest danger to you, and how does this passage help you to avoid that danger?

pray

Spend some time in confession—either in silence or out loud. Conclude these prayers with the promise of **1 John 1 v 8-9**. Having reflected both on the depth of sin and God's wonderful promise of forgiveness, finish the session in praise to God, and prayers for the greatest need of non-Christians—forgiveness of their sins.

10 "I believe in ... the resurrection of the body, and the life everlasting"

THE HOPE OF THE SPIRIT

Romans 8 v 18-39

talkabout

1. What do you imagine heaven or eternal life will be like?

investigate

Read Romans 8 v 18-22

2. What has happened to the created world as a result of humanity's rejection of God?

DICTIONARY

Bondage (v 21): slavery.

In verse 19 Paul tells us that the whole of creation is waiting for a time in the future when the sons of God will be revealed—those who belong to Christ will be given eternal life (v 11) and will share in Christ's glory (v 17). In other words, God will make a new humanity.

3. What will happen to the created world as a result of God's new humanity?

Read verses 23-27

4. What are Christians waiting for? (See also verse 11.)

> **DICTIONARY**
>
> **Intercedes for (v 26, 27):** speaks on behalf of.

5. What do we learn about the life of eternity from verses 18-27?

6. What does Paul mean when he says Christians have "the firstfruits of the Spirit" (v 23)?

7. How does the Spirit help us as we wait for our final redemption?

apply

8. God is going to give Christians renewed physical bodies in a renewed physical world (v 21, 23). How should this affect our attitude to our bodies and the physical world now?

9. In verses 24-25, Paul says we are waiting for our redemption. What happens if you think you will receive complete health, justice or prosperity in this life, rather than in the life to come?

investigate

Read verses 28-39

10. What is God's plan for Christians?

DICTIONARY

Conformed to the image of (v 29): changed to be like.

11. Why can Christians be confident about the future?
- v 23:

- v 28-30:

- v 31-34:

• v 35-39:

optional

explore more

List the main questions that Paul asks in Romans 8 v 31-39.

How does he answer each question?

apply

12. What difference should our future resurrection to everlasting life in glory make to the way we live now?

13. Look back over the whole passage. How should these verses help Christians who are suffering?

14. Paul reminds us in verse 7 that we are made right with God by His grace. But we still do wrong things. Being changed by the Holy Spirit is a process. What happens if we forget it is a process?

getting personal

Sooner or later you will face suffering—are you prepared for it?

Will you then be able to consider present suffering "not worth comparing" with future glory? Are you already living a life that is different from those around you, because every day you look forward to your eternal life? What can you do now to prepare for suffering?

pray

Think of Christians you know who are struggling at the moment. Identify a verse from Romans 8 that speaks to their situation and use it as the basis for a prayer on their behalf.

As this is the final session, why not read through the Apostles' Creed together? Spend some time thanking God for what you have learned, and praying for each other, that God would help you all to live according to His glorious truth.

I believe

The Apostles' Creed

LEADER'S GUIDE

Leader's Guide

INTRODUCTION

Leading a Bible study can be a bit like herding cats—everyone has a different idea of what the passage could be about, and a different line of enquiry that they want to pursue. But a good group leader is more than someone who just referees this kind of discussion. You will want to:

- correctly understand and handle the Bible passage. But also...
- encourage and train the people in your group to do this for themselves. Don't fall into the trap of spoon-feeding people by simply passing on the information in the Leader's Guide. Then...
- make sure that no Bible study is finished without everyone knowing how the passage is relevant for them. What changes do you all need to make in the light of the things you have been learning? And finally...
- encourage the group to turn all that has been learned and discussed into prayer.

Your Bible-study group is unique, and you are likely to know better than anyone the capabilities, backgrounds and circumstances of the people you are leading. That's why we've designed these guides with a number of optional features. If they're a quiet bunch, you might want to spend longer on talkabout. If your time is limited, you can choose to skip explore more, or get people to look at these questions at home. Can't get enough of Bible study? Well, some studies have optional extra homework projects. As leader, you can adapt and select the material to the needs of your particular group.

So what's in the Leader's Guide?

The main thing that this Leader's Guide will help you to do is to understand the major teaching points in the passage you are studying, and how to apply them. As well as guidance on the questions, the Leader's Guide for each session contains the following important sections:

THE BIG IDEA

One key sentence will give you the main point of the session. This is what you should be aiming to have fixed in people's minds as they leave the Bible study. And it's the point you need to head back towards when the discussion goes off at a tangent.

SUMMARY

An overview of the passage, including plenty of useful historical background information.

OPTIONAL EXTRA

Usually this is an introductory activity that ties in with the main theme of the Bible study, and is designed to "break the ice" at the beginning of a session. Or it may be a "homework project" that people can tackle during the week.

So let's take a look at the various different features of a Good Book Guide:

talkabout

Each session kicks off with a discussion question, based on the group's opinions or experiences. It's designed to get people talking and thinking in a general way about the main subject of the Bible study.

investigate

The first thing you and your group need to know is what the Bible passage is about, which is the purpose of these questions. But watch out—people may come up with answers based on their experiences or teaching they have heard in the past, without referring to the passage at all. It's amazing how often we can get through a Bible study without actually looking at the Bible! If you're stuck for an answer, the Leader's Guide contains guidance on questions. These are the answers to direct your group to. This information isn't meant to be read out to people—ideally, you want them to discover these answers from the Bible for themselves. Sometimes there are optional follow-up questions (see ⊻ in guidance on questions) to help you help your group get to the answer.

explore more

These questions generally point people to other relevant parts of the Bible. They are useful for helping your group to see how the passage fits into the "big picture" of the whole Bible. These sections are OPTIONAL—only use them if you have time. Remember that it's better to finish in good time having really grasped one big thing from the passage, than to try and cram everything in.

apply

We want to encourage you to spend more time working at application—too often, it is simply tacked on at the end. In the Good Book Guides, apply sections are mixed in with the investigate sections of the study. We hope that people will realise that application is not just an optional extra, but rather, the whole purpose of studying the Bible. We do Bible study so that our lives can be changed by what we hear from God's word. If you skip the application, the Bible study hasn't achieved its purpose.

These questions draw out practical lessons that we can all learn from the Bible passage. You can review what has been learned so far, and think about practical differences that this should make in our churches and our lives. The group gets the opportunity to talk about what they personally have learned.

getting personal

These can be done at home, but it is well worth allowing a few moments of quiet reflection during the study for each person to think and pray about specific changes they need to make in their own lives. Why not have a time for reporting back at the beginning of the following session, so that everyone can be encouraged and challenged by one another to make application a priority?

pray

In Acts 4 v 25-30 the first Christians quoted Psalm 2 as they prayed in response to the persecution of the apostles by the Jewish religious leaders. Today however, it's not as common for Christians to base prayers on the truths of God's word as it once was. As a result, our prayers tend to be weak, superficial and self-centred rather than bold, visionary and God-centred.

The prayer section is based on what has been learned from the Bible passage. How different our prayer times would be if we were genuinely responding to what God has said to us through His word.

1 Romans 1 v 18-25; John 14 v 1-14

BELIEVING IN GOD

THE BIG IDEA

We can know God because He has graciously revealed Himself in the world, in His Son and in His word. The fear of the Lord is the beginning of knowledge.

SUMMARY

The aim of this first session is to confidently proclaim the teaching of the Bible, that God does indeed exist (in fact, it is irrational to believe that He doesn't), and that we can know Him, but only as we treat Him like God and accept what He tells us about Himself.

In Romans 1 Paul says God has revealed Himself in the world around us. This is called "natural revelation". But people do not believe in God because they do not want to worship Him. They suppress the truth and so their minds become darkened. The problem is not that people cannot know God—what may be known about God is plain, says Paul. The problem is that people will not know God. They choose to worship what is created, instead of submitting to the Creator. It is a relational problem rather than an intellectual problem—a heart problem rather than a head problem.

The same principle continues to apply to Christians. If we refuse to submit to God in some way, then we will tend to misunderstand or distort the truth (see 1 Timothy 1 v 5-7, 18-20). "The fear of the Lord is the beginning of knowledge, but fools despise wisdom and instruction" (Proverbs 1 v 7). So if the Apostles' Creed is simply recited, but not lived, then its truths will inevitably become twisted in our sinful, darkened minds.

In John 14 we learn that God has revealed Himself supremely in His Son (v 6), whose identity was confirmed by His miracles (v 11). We know God the Father through God the Son (v 7-9). The words of Jesus reveal God (v 10). So even though we cannot see Jesus now, His words still reveal God to us. The words of Jesus also do the work of God (v 10)—God works through His word. Jesus says Christians will do greater works than He did (v 12-14). He has already defined these greater works as giving eternal life to His people (John 5 v 19-24). As Christians prayerfully proclaim the word of God, God gives eternal life through faith in Jesus.

Key issues: revelation, Jesus' identity, God's work of salvation, faith, the Bible.

OPTIONAL EXTRA

You could begin this series by talking about the Apostles' Creed. You may say it regularly in your church. Ask people how they feel about it. Has it become part of your lives? Do you take it for granted? What do you think about when you are reciting it? Are there phrases in the Creed that puzzle you? Do you think reciting a creed is a valuable thing to do? Does saying the Creed on Sunday affect your life on Monday? You might read through the history of the Creed in the introduction at this point.

GUIDANCE ON QUESTIONS

1. What reasons do people give about why they don't believe in God? What do you think makes it hard for people to believe in God? If people want to talk personally, then let them do so, but do not force this. The purpose of the talkabout section is to raise questions, rather than to provide answers at this stage. This particular question prepares the ground for understanding that there is a discrepancy between the reasons people give for their lack of belief in God, and the true reason.

- **What reasons lead you to believe that God is real?** Again, there are no wrong answers at this stage.

2. According to Paul, how has God made Himself known? In the world He has made. See also Psalm 19 v 1-6.

3. What does Paul say we can know about God from creation? The visible world reveals God's invisible qualities. The world shows us something of God's "eternal power and divine nature" (v 20). In other words, we can see that there is a God and that He rules over the world. (**Note:** This does not mean that we can find out everything about God from creation.) Paul also says this revelation is "plain" (v 19) and can be "clearly seen", so people are "without excuse" (v 20).

4. According to Paul, why don't people believe in God? You might preface this question by drawing attention to the fact that revelation is plain and clear (v 19-20). But people suppress the truth (v 18). Their hearts are darkened because they refuse to worship God or give thanks to Him (v 21). The problem is not that people cannot know God: the problem is that people will not know God—it is a problem of the heart rather than a problem of the head.

5. APPLY: Look at verse 21. If we want to get to know God or understand Him better, where must we start? Verse 21 says that our thinking becomes futile and our minds darkened when we refuse to glorify God or give Him thanks. This is the natural state of everyone before becoming a Christian. So the first thing we need to do, in order to get to know God, is to glorify Him and give Him thanks. This principle continues to apply to Christians as well. If there is still some way in which we refuse to submit to God, then we will tend to misunderstand or distort the truth (see 1 Timothy 1 v 5-7, 18-20). The same will be true if we do not give thanks to Him, but instead, question His goodness in our lives. Proverbs 1 v 7 says: "The fear of the Lord is the beginning of knowledge, but fools despise wisdom and instruction". To begin to know and understand God, we need to have a right relationship to God of worship and submission. The Apostles' Creed is not simply to be recited, but lived.

EXPLORE MORE
What are the implications for us as Christians, when we try to convince people of the truth of Christianity? In Romans 1 Paul says that people do not believe in God because of their godlessness and wickedness (v 18)—they do not want to obey Him. So while intellectual argument about God's existence may have a place, it does not address the central problem.
Read Deut 4 v 5-8; 1 Peter 2 v 11-12. How were God's people, in both the Old and New Testaments, to bring unbelieving people to believe in the one true God? How might this help us convince people who suppress the truth because they will not obey God? In both the Old and New Testaments, God's people were to show by their lives how good it is to live in obedience to God. Christians are to show that God's rule is a good rule

that brings life, justice, freedom and hope. We are to show how good it is to live in relationship with God.

6. According to Jesus, how can we know God? Jesus says we can only know God through Him. See verses 6, 7, 9, 10 and 11.

7. What does Jesus mean when He describes Himself as "the way and the truth and the life" (v 6)? This question reinforces the truth that we can know God through Jesus. The three images engage us at an emotional level, so spend time in thinking about what each image means. Without Jesus, we are lost, ignorant and dead. Explore this in general terms and then apply to our knowledge of God. You might ask: Have you ever been lost on a journey? Did you ever get lost as a child? How did it feel? And so on.

8. Jesus tells His disciples that anyone who has seen Him has seen the Father (v 9). But how can people who have not seen Jesus (like us!) know the Father? (See verse 10 and compare John 20 v 29-31.) *Verse 10:* we cannot see Jesus, but we do have the words of Jesus. *John 20 v 29-31:* John has written down the words of (and about) Jesus so that those who have never met Him physically will nevertheless believe that He is the Christ, the Son of God.

9. What does Jesus say about His words in v 10? That they come from the Father.

- **What does He say about the Father's work?** That the Father does His work through the words of Jesus. We expect Jesus to say: "The words I say to you are not just my own. Rather, it is the Father, living in me, who is speaking His words." But in fact, Jesus says: "… doing His work". You could read out verse 10 without the ending and ask how we would expect it to end.

- **So how does God do His work today?** Through the words of Jesus, which are proclaimed by Christians. Be aware that some people may have very different ideas about how God works in our world today; for example, bringing about world peace, or fairer societies and communities, through individuals or political structures. Rather than getting side-tracked into these issues, emphasise that John clearly teaches here that God's work is done through Jesus' words. To find out what God achieves through His work (see next question), people need to know what Jesus has said.

10. Look at John 5 v 19-24. What does the work of God, through the words of Jesus, actually do in this world? When people hear and believe the words of Jesus, God gives them eternal life and they will not be judged (v 21, 24).

11. In John 14 v 12, Jesus says that those who have faith in Him will do greater works than the miracles He did. How do Christians do the "greater works" that Jesus promises? In two ways. First, we proclaim the message of Jesus to the whole world. To help people see this, get them to recall how God does His work in verse 10—through the words of Jesus. Secondly, we pray (v 13-14). Our job is prayerfully to proclaim the message of Jesus.

- **What should we pray for and why?** We pray that people with darkened hearts

(Romans 1 v 21) might recognise Jesus as the truth of God (John 14 v 6). We do this because it is God who does the greater work of giving eternal life when people believe in Jesus.

12. APPLY: What do your friends and colleagues think about how God can be known, and how He works in the world? Some may not think there is a God to be known. Others may think God cannot be known. Others may think God can be known through spiritual experiences or religious activity. Many will think all religions lead to God. They may claim it is arrogant to think only Christianity is true.

13. APPLY: How could you use Romans 1 and John 14 to respond to these beliefs? We cannot know God by being clever enough, good enough, religious enough or spiritual enough to discover the truth about Him. We can only know God because He has graciously revealed Himself in His world, His Son and His word. It is not arrogant to claim to know God through Jesus—we admit we cannot know God through what we do, but we depend on God's gracious revelation in His Son.

Those who say all religions lead to God have to make sense of the differences between religions. If pressed, most people say that the true "god" behind religions either can't be known or is impersonal. But Jesus Christ has made God known—God has come to us in the person of the Son, and the Son shows us the Father. If you looked at the Explore More on Deuteronomy 4 v 5-8 and 1 Peter 2 v 11-12, you may also want to press home its relevance at this point.

---

2 John 17 v 20-26 THE TRIUNE GOD

THE BIG IDEA

God is one being with three persons, which means God both reigns over the universe and is intimately involved in our lives.

SUMMARY

This session investigates one fundamental aspect of what God has revealed about Himself in the words of Jesus—that He is three persons in one being: the Trinity.

God is one being with three persons. The Bible says God is a divine community of Father, Son and Holy Spirit. The Father, Son and Spirit are defined by their love for each other. The Father is the Father because He has a Son and so on. But they not only share one love, they also share one being. Jesus, speaking to the Father, says: "You are in me and I am in you" (John 17 v 21).

The Trinity is not a closed community. The Father sent the Son into the world and the Son sends the Spirit into the world from the Father. And God invites us to share the life of the Trinity. We become part of God's family. Because God is triune, He can simultaneously reign over us, live among us and live within us.

People today often try to "find themselves" by being different from other people ("expressing their individuality"). But divine personhood is defined by relationships. God the Father is a Father because He has a Son. And we are made in the image of the triune God. This means that we are designed to find our identity through relationships—as children, husbands and wives, parents, friends and, above all, as children of God in fellowship with our brothers and sisters. We cannot "find ourselves" by abandoning these relationships.

Jesus says that people will believe in the triune God through the unity of His people. The Christian community is what will persuade people that God is triune.

Key issues: the Trinity, humanity, mission.

OPTIONAL EXTRA

Do you know someone who was drawn to the truth about God because they witnessed the love and unity of Christians? Invite this person to share their testimony with your group—it may be one of your participants or a guest. You could interview this person live, or make a recording, or read out a written testimony. Or perhaps you have come across a story like this in a Christian biography or autobiography that you could share with your group.

GUIDANCE ON QUESTIONS

1. How would you answer the question "'Who are you?" Think of a few different endings to the following sentence that will give true descriptions of yourself: I am... If you wish, you could get people to write down some endings to the sentence. Stress that they should be brief and fairly immediate responses. Then go round the group and see how many have identified themselves in terms of relationships eg: I am... the husband of Sarah, the mother of two teenagers, a member of (insert name) church, a citizen of the UK, a forgiven child of God etc.

This question aims to show people how important relationships are in defining our identity, and prepares the ground for understanding that this is how we are designed because we have been made in the image of God, who has always existed in relationship within the Trinity.

However, it doesn't matter if people haven't described themselves in these terms, since we also live in a highly individualistic society, which influences all of us to define ourselves in terms of our achievements or ambitions, rather than our relationships.

2. What does Jesus say about His relationship with the Father? Jesus is in the Father and the Father is in Jesus (v 21, 23). The Father sent Jesus into the world (v 21, 23, 25) and Jesus makes the Father known (v 26). The Father loves the Son (v 23, 24, 26) and glorifies Him (v 22, 24).

3. How long has the Father loved the Son? From before the creation of the world (v 24).

4. What does this tell us about Jesus?

- **How is Jesus different from us?** Jesus existed before God made all things. He is not part of creation. Jesus was not made by God at a moment in time. The Father and Son have always existed together in eternal love.
- **1 John 4 v 8 tells us that "God is love". Could this statement be true if God existed on His own before creation? Why or why not?** To love there must be someone or something that can be loved. God could not be love

if He was on His own before time began, because there would be nothing else to be loved. However, God has always loved because He has always existed as a loving community of three persons loving each other.

5. Jesus says the Trinity is like a loving family ... What does He say that suggests the Trinity is more than a family of separate individuals? The Son is in the Father and the Father is in the Son (v 21, 23). People may have identified this when answering Q2, but now we want to highlight the implications. You may want to ask: "What does this tell us about the Father and the Son?" The Father and Son share one being. In theological language, the persons of the Trinity mutually indwell one another—something theologians call "perichoresis". It is difficult for us to understand how different persons can share one being or nature, but this is what the Bible says God is like.

Note: Some people may get "stuck" at this point, feeling that they have to understand the Bible teaching of the Trinity, but unable to truly grasp it. Point out that, as finite creatures, it is vital to accept that we can never understand everything about the infinite God. However, it is thrilling that God has chosen to reveal so much of Himself to humanity. We may not be able to understand everything but the question is: can we trust God and what He says? Acting on trust, rather than understanding, is something we do in many areas of life eg: following medical treatment, following instructions for using a computer etc. As we learn about God in the Bible, we find that there are supremely good grounds for trusting what He has revealed about Himself. (See also question 11 below, on how Christians are to convince people that God is triune.)

6. Jesus describes the Holy Spirit as "the Counsellor" or "the Helper". What does He say about the Father's relationship with the Spirit? The Spirit "goes out from the Father" (15 v 26; see also 14 v 26). The Spirit makes known what the Son has received from the Father (16 v 15).

7. In the same verses, what does Jesus say about His own relationship with the Spirit? The Son sends the Spirit from the Father and the Spirit testifies about the Son (15 v 26). The Spirit ensures that the testimony of the apostles—which we have in the New Testament—is true (16 v 13; see also 2 Timothy 3 v 16). The Spirit brings glory to the Son by making Him known (16 v 14; see also 16 v 7-10).

8. APPLY: How does the triune God of the Bible differ from many commonly-held beliefs about God? Encourage people to share different understandings about God that they have come across, either in conversation with people they know or from what they have heard on radio and TV, from other religions etc. For instance, many people think of God as just a creative force or energy in the universe; Muslims believe there is only one God, but they also refuse to accept that He can be in three persons—the Koran says that He is above having a son (4.171); eastern religions tend to regard emotions and feelings as human weaknesses—which we should seek to rise above, in order to attain serenity—and so deny that God loves or "is love".

- **How would you respond to someone who says that all religions lead to the same God?** The teaching that God is triune is unique to Christianity. A clear implication will be that all religions don't lead to the same God. Christians should be encouraged to challenge people with this fact and the question "Who then is the true God?"

EXPLORE MORE

Read Ephesians 1 v 3-14 ... What is the role of the Father in salvation? He planned our salvation—He chose us and loved us before He made the world (v 4). He has adopted us as His own children through Jesus Christ (v 5).

What is the role of the Son? He achieved our salvation by dying in our place—He redeemed us through His blood so that our sins could be forgiven (v 7). We messed up this world because of our sin, but God is going to bring everything together under Christ.

And what is the role of the Spirit? He applies salvation to our hearts and lives—He enables us to respond to the gospel message with faith (v 13). He seals us, or keeps us, while we wait for Jesus to return (v 13-14). And the Spirit gives us a foretaste of heaven.

- **What do you notice in verses 6, 12 and 14?** At the end of each section, Paul says "to the praise of his glorious grace" or "glory" (v 6, 12, 14). Father, Son and Spirit planned salvation to bring one another glory. Believers are part of God's plan to glorify Himself!

9. What does this tell us about the Trinity? The Trinity has a mission. The word "mission" comes from the Latin word "to send". It was not until the 16th century that it was used to talk about Christian witness. Before that it was always used of the Trinity. "Mission" describes what God does to save His people by sending the Son and the Spirit into the world.

10. How does Jesus describe the relationship between the Trinity and Christian believers in John 17 v 20-26? Christians will be in the Father and in the Son (v 21). And the Son will be in us (v 23, 26). Christians share the glory of Jesus, which the Father has given Him (v 22). And Christians share the love of Jesus, which the Father has shown Him (v 23). Christians will be with Jesus and see His glory (v 24). Jesus makes the Father known to Christians so they might share God's love (v 26). In other words, Christians share the life and love of the Trinity. The Trinity is not a closed community because we are part of the family!

11. How will the world come to believe in God? Look at verses 21 and 23. The world will believe in the triune God through the unity of believers.

- **What is it about God that the world will believe?** That the Father sent the Son. In other words, that Jesus is the divine Son of God, sent into the world by the Father. We often struggle to explain the Trinity to people. Jesus says the Christian community is what will persuade people that God is triune.

EXPLORE MORE

On the cross, who was the sacrifice and to whom was the sacrifice offered? God the Son (Jesus) was the sacrifice and God the Father was the one to whom the sacrifice was offered (Hebrews 9 v 14). In other words, God offered Himself to

Himself.

Who was judged and who did the judging? (See also Isaiah 53 v 4-6—an Old Testament prophecy of Jesus' death on the cross.) The judge and the judged were one being. God judged God.

God could truly deal with our sin at the cross only because He is triune. Can you explain why? If God were not triune, then God would have cruelly punished an innocent victim on the cross. But God Himself bore His own anger against our sin. You could also ask people about he role of the Spirit at the cross. It is not clear what it means when it says Jesus offered Himself "through the eternal Spirit" (Hebrews 9 v 14). The Spirit empowered Jesus for His ministry (see Luke 4 v 14), so it may be that, in a similar way, the Spirit empowered Jesus to offer Himself on the cross.

12. APPLY: How might you use the Bible's teaching on the Trinity to advise:

- **a woman who is about to leave her marriage because she wants to "find herself"?**
- **a student who thinks he can be a Christian without going to church?**
- **a young man who will not get married for fear of losing his freedom?**
- **a woman who feels tied down by her responsibilities to her ageing parents?**

In the Bible, the word "person" is understood in the same way as the words "mother" or "friend"—the idea makes no sense without a relationship with other people. Just as you cannot have a "childless mother", so you cannot have a person without relationships. We are dehumanised if we abandon our responsibilities to others. You should, however, explore these issues with pastoral sensitivity. There may, for example, be situations in which a woman should leave a violent or abusive husband.

13. APPLY: Jesus says the world will believe in the triune God as it sees the Christian community (v 21 and 23). When do unbelievers see the life of your Christian church or group? How can you ensure that outsiders see more of your love for one another? This passage is sometimes used to justify moves to institutional unity in the church. But Jesus is talking about something that can be seen on the ground, so focus the discussion on your church or Christian group. It might involve planning social events or meals together as a group to which friends can be invited.

---

3 Psalm 33
THE SOVEREIGN GOD

THE BIG IDEA

God is the Creator, who rules over His world through His word, and He is also the Father, who watches over His people in love.

SUMMARY

Psalm 33 weaves together the themes of creation, God's reign and God's care of His people. The Creed affirms that the world was made by God. It did not come about by chance, nor is it part of God (though God is everywhere in it). God made the universe as something separate from Him and dependent on Him. But the biblical doctrine of creation is more than an abstract theory of how things came to be. It is about how the world belongs to God the Creator and how we are accountable to Him. It is about how God the Creator continues to rule over the world and to care for His people in love. All these themes are in Psalm 33.

Verses 1-5 are a call to praise God (v 1-3). We praise God because of who He is; because of His word, His faithfulness, His justice and His love (v 4-5). The rest of the psalm expounds these divine characteristics.

1. The creating word of God (v 6-9). God created the world and He created it by His word. Christians disagree on whether the world was made in six 24-hour days or whether creation involved some form of evolution over longer periods of time. But, whatever the process, we can affirm that God made the world out of nothing, by His word.
2. The unchanging plan of God (v 10-12). God rules over the world. Human beings cannot alter God's plan. Verse 12 tells us that God's plan has a particular focus: to save people who will become His people. Just as God created through His word, so He also rules through His word. All authority has been given to Jesus, and Jesus extends His reign as we proclaim God's word and call on people to obey that word (Matthew 28 v 18-20).
3. The loving look of God (v 13-19). In verses 13-15 the writer says that God "sees", "watches" and "considers". And three times he uses the word "all". God sees all things, even our hearts. Verses 16-17 then repeat the word "great" three times ("by the size of his army" in the NIV is literally "by his great army"). Human greatness cannot deliver—certainly not from the all-seeing judgment of the Creator. Verses 18-19 bring together the two ideas of God's all-seeing gaze and the inability of human greatness to deliver. But God watches over His people in love (see v 5, 18, 22) and He delivers them from death.

Verses 20-22 tell us that we should respond with hope in God. The Creator God is the almighty Ruler of history. So when we face difficult times, we can trust Him. He is our Help and our Shield. He will keep us and deliver us—if not in this life, then in the life to come.

Key issues: God, creation, providence, the kingdom of God, suffering.

OPTIONAL EXTRA

God made a good world for us to enjoy (Gen 1 v 31; 1 Tim 4 v 4). Even though our sin has spoilt God's world, we still see much of God's goodness in the world. Invite some of the group to talk about what they find good in the world God has made. It might be a person, a place or an activity. They may want to bring an object, picture, photo or poem. Celebrate together the good world that God has created.

GUIDANCE TO QUESTIONS

1. Have you ever struggled to believe that God is in control of events? This question may touch upon some people's most painful inner struggles. They may be unwilling to share these, especially if your group has not yet built up a strong level of trust. Do not force the issue. The question will hopefully get people applying the psalm to their personal struggles, even if they do not share these with the group.

2. Why should we sing joyfully to the LORD? Make sure people answer this question by looking at the psalm. Verses 1-3 describe how we should praise God. Verse 4 begins with the word "For". It introduces the reasons why we should praise God. Verses 4-5 give four reasons: God's word is true, He is always faithful, He is committed to justice and His love is everywhere.

3. How do life's difficulties cause us to doubt what this psalm says about God in v 4-5? Work through each statement in v 4-5. We may doubt that God's word is true (for example, we may doubt that God is in control or that God graciously accepts us in Christ). We may doubt that God is faithful to His promises. We may doubt God's commitment to justice when we say things like "It's not fair". We may think that God's love does not reach into our situation.

- **What happens when we do not believe that God is like this?** We lose our joy (v 1 and 3; see also James 1 v 2-4).

4. How does the psalm describe God's work of creation? *The scope of God's work of creation:* As the Creed puts it, He is the "creator of heaven and earth". Notice how the psalm highlights those parts of creation that are still beyond the reach of humanity—the stars (v 6) and the depths of the oceans (v 7). *The power of God's work of creation:* Encourage people to enjoy the imagery that the psalm uses in verses 6-7. Creating is no more difficult for God than a simple breath (v 6) or filling a jar with water (v 7). (See also Isaiah 40 v 12-17.) *The way in which God creates:* He creates by His word. "He spoke, and it came to be" (v 9). This is how Genesis 1 also describes the creation of all things. "And God said, 'Let there be light,' and there was light" (Genesis 1 v 3).

- **What does the rest of the Bible teach about the involvement of the Trinity in creation (see John 1 v 1-3 and Genesis 1 v 1-2)?** *John 1 v 1-3:* Jesus was "the Word", by which God created all things. *Genesis 1 v 1-2:* mentions the presence of the Spirit at creation.
Note: The word "breath" in Psalm 33 v 6 could also be translated "Spirit". The Word of God came on the breath of God. The whole Trinity was involved in creation.

5. What is the right way for us to respond to God the Creator? Look at v 8.

6. How is God involved in the world He has made? Look at v 10-11. God rules over the world. He is "almighty", as the Creed puts it. God foils human plans when they are contrary to His sovereign will. People cannot alter God's plan. His purposes always succeed. The theological term for this is "omnipotence" = all-powerful.

7. What is the focus of God's plan for history (v 12)? God has chosen a group of people for His inheritance. This verse reflects the teaching of the rest of the Bible—that the focus of God's plan is to save people, so that they will become His people.

- **Who are these people?** Read Exodus 19 v 3-6: In the Old Testament, God's people were Israel, the nation that He rescued from slavery in Egypt, to whom He gave His law and the land that He had promised them. See 1 Peter 2 v 9: In the New Testament, Christians are God's people. The church is now God's chosen nation and His inheritance.

8. APPLY: Think over what we have learned so far about God from Psalm 33. How do people often get God wrong? Take your group through the things that we have learned about God so far, and by contrast with each point, discuss how non-Christians may view God instead.

There are many things that Psalm 33 tells us about God that non-Christians do not know or believe. For example:

- knowing God brings us joy (v 1-3), but non-Christians often think that knowing God makes you solemn or strict or dull.
- God has spoken to this world (v 4), but non-Christians often imagine that God is distant and no longer involved with His creation.
- God intervenes in the plans of political leaders (v 10), but this is not apparent to non-Christians. Nor is the fact that God has His own plans, which He is working out through history (v 11).
- God's plans focus on the people He has chosen (v 12), but non-Christians tend only to see the church as insignificant, irrelevant and outdated.
- When non-Christians see suffering and disasters, they often believe that God is either not powerful enough or not interested enough to stop them.
- Non-Christians themselves choose how they will live, because they imagine that God isn't very interested in what they do, or that He will forgive them anyway.
- **What do we need to make clear about God as we speak to others? (See Acts 17 v 22-31 for an example of how the apostle Paul speaks about the one Creator God to a multi-faith society.)** Take your group again through the things that we have learned about God so far, and share thoughts on how Christians might proclaim these truths clearly to those around them. People may have had experiences of being able to communicate to others something of God's almighty power or unfailing love, when they were going through a difficult time. Challenge your group to think about whether they give a false impression of God to others (eg: He is weak or uncaring).

9. What do verses 13-15 say about God's relationship to the world? Each verse says something similar: that God watches over all He has made. The psalm says God "looks down", "sees", "watches" and "considers". And three times it says "all". God knows all things—even the thoughts of our hearts. The theological term for this is "omniscience" = all-knowing. Notice the link in v 15 between the fact that God is the Creator and the fact that He is all-seeing. These verses suggest we are accountable to God. Our Creator watches all we do and think, and we are accountable to Him (v 8).

10. What do verses 16-17 say about humanity? Verses 16-17 repeat the word "great" three times ("by the size of his army" in the NIV is literally "by his great army"). Human greatness cannot guarantee deliverance. And it can never deliver us from the all-seeing judgment of our Creator.

11. The Creator God is all-powerful and all-seeing. What does this mean for those who do not trust Him? See verses 8, 10, 15, 16-17. People should fear God. They cannot prevent His plans. They are accountable to Him, and He sees all they do and think. No one can deliver them from His judgment.

- **What does this mean for His people?** Look at verses 18-19. God watches over the world to hold people to account, but God watches over His people in love (v 5, 18, 22). God's all-seeing eyes are a threat to the ungodly, but a comfort to His people. Human greatness cannot deliver, but God Himself delivers His people. The fact that God is all-powerful ("omnipotent") and all-seeing ("omniscient") is not a threat to His people. It is their hope. God may not always deliver us in the way we'd like, but He will deliver us from death. **Note:** If your group is not familiar with the Bible, you may like to discuss the following questions:

- **Verse 19 tells us that God will deliver His people from death. But what does this mean for Christians living in a world where everyone will die? See 1 Corinthians 15 v 21-26.**
- **How does God deliver His people from death? See Hebrews 2 v 9, 14-15.**

12. How does this psalm invite us to respond to the truth that God is the almighty Creator of heaven and earth? The psalm invites us to hope in God and to trust in Him (v 20-21). The powerful reign of the Creator God should make our hearts rejoice (v 21 and v 1-3). The psalm also invites us to pray to God. Verse 22 is in the form of a prayer. To bring this out you could ask: "What's different about verse 22?" "To whom is it speaking?" Verse 5 says the earth is full of God's unfailing love and verse 18 says God watches over His people in His unfailing love. Now the writer prays for God's unfailing love to rest upon us.

EXPLORE MORE

Read Matthew 6 v 25-34. How does Jesus describe God's relationship with His people? As their heavenly Father. **What does this relationship mean for Christians? Look at the following passages to find out: Matthew 5 v 43-48; 6 v 5-8; 6 v 9-15; 7 v 7-12.**

- *5 v 43-48:* Christians are called to take after their heavenly Father.
- *6 v 5-8:* Christians should not want to impress others eg: in the way they pray, but to please their heavenly Father.
- *6 v 9-15:* Christians can and should pray to their heavenly Father in the way modelled by Jesus.
- *7 v 7-12:* Christians can be confident in approaching God with requests, and can trust Him to give only good gifts.

13. APPLY: If Psalm 33 is true, why does God allow bad things to happen to His children? (See also Romans 8 v 28-30 and John 9 v 1-3.) God uses suffering to make us more like Jesus (Romans 8 v 28-30) and to bring Him glory (John 9 v 1-3). Suffering also reminds us that we live in a sin-spoilt world that has not yet been put right (Romans 8 v 18-25). It helps us to stop living for this life that will pass away, and live instead for the glorious life to come in eternity. We also find comfort in the fact that God has suffered with us (Mark 15 v 34 and Hebrews 4 v 15).

- **Read Romans 8 v 28-30: What does God promise to do for His people in every situation?** To work for our good.
- **What is God's purpose for His people (v 29)? To make us like His Son, Jesus.**
- **Read John 11 v 1-4. According to Jesus, what was the reason why God had allowed Lazarus to get sick?** This situation would bring glory to God and His Son. Jesus would be seen raising Lazarus to life again (v 43-44)—proof of His words

to Martha, that He is the resurrection and the life (v 25-26), and the reason why many people put their faith in Him (v 45).

14. APPLY: What should we remind one another of when we face difficulties in life? We can remind one another that God is the Creator, who rules over His creation. We can remind one another of God's character (v 4-5). We can remind one another that God watches over His people in love. He sees our problems (v 13-15, 18). We cannot deliver, but God does deliver us—if not in this life, then in the life to come (v 19). This question is a chance to summarise what the psalm teaches, but also to apply it to our hearts. You might like to create some real-life scenarios or case studies. "What would you say to ...?"

---

4 Hebrews 1 – 2
THE IDENTITY OF JESUS CHRIST

THE BIG IDEA

Jesus, who is fully God, became fully human to restore humanity's rule over God's world, and to set us free from the fear of death and the guilt of sin.

SUMMARY

Two false views of Jesus are commonly held by religious people. Some see Jesus simply as their personal Saviour—they have little understanding of the big picture of salvation, or of Jesus' role in God's plan of restoration for the entire universe. Others have little understanding of the humanity of Jesus and its implications—they view Jesus as a remote figure, who is too holy and exalted to be approached directly in prayer. This session will show that both these views of Jesus are false.

The letter of Hebrews is written to encourage its readers to keep going as Christians. It does this by showing how wonderful Jesus is, and all He has achieved.

Chapter 1 tells us that Jesus is the Son of God, God's ultimate revelation, the Maker of all things and the exact representation of God's being. Jesus is fully God and God's only eternal Son. The chapter also says that Jesus is the promised Messiah, and shows from the Old Testament that the promised Messiah is superior to the angels, for He will rule over God's kingdom for ever.

Chapter 2 is about the humanity of Jesus. Jesus may be superior to the angels in ability and status, but Jesus was made a little lower than the angels—He became fully human. Through His humanity:

- Jesus restores humanity's rule over God's world as the new Adam (v 5-9);
- Jesus enables God's people to become God's family, with Jesus as our brother (v 10-13);
- Jesus died as our representative and so frees us from the fear of death and turns away God's judgment against our sin (v 14-17);
- Jesus helps us when we struggle with sin (v 18).

Note: In their original contexts, the Old Testament quotations in 2 v 12-13a both speak of Christ's death and the benefits for those He represents.

- V 12 is a quotation from Psalm 22 v 22. The first half of the psalm describes the sufferings of God's King. It begins with the words that Jesus quoted on the cross: "My God, my God, why have you forsaken me?" The verse quoted in Hebrews 2 v 12 begins the second half of the psalm, which speaks of the resulting glory and blessings for God's people.
- V 13a is a quotation from Isaiah 8 v 17. The prophet says he will trust in God in the face of the faithlessness of God's people and God's judgment on them. Those who share his faith are the children of God. Jesus is the ultimate faithful servant of God. He was faithful right through to His death. As a result, God gives Him many children (= members of God's family).

Key issues: the divinity and humanity of Christ, incarnation, humanity, salvation.

OPTIONAL EXTRA

Ask people to write down the jobs or roles of three of their relatives—the more unusual the better. Read out each person's list and see if the group can guess whose it is. Discuss to what degree people think their families have shaped their identity. Hebrews 1 v 3 says that Jesus is the exact representation of God's being. There is a perfect family resemblance! Hebrews 2 v 11-13 says that Christians are now part of God's family. We have a new family identity. What about a new family resemblance?

GUIDANCE ON QUESTIONS

1. What does our culture think about Jesus? Many believe that Jesus was only "a good man" or "a man of peace". Others are willing to call Him "Son of God". But be aware that this doesn't necessarily mean that people understand who Jesus is—they may simply be using a familiar term, without any understanding of what it means.

2. What does the writer say about Jesus? And about the relationship of Jesus to God the Father? Jesus is the way God ultimately reveals Himself (v 1-2)—the divine Son, the Heir of all things and the Maker of the universe (v 2), and also the exact representation of the Father's being (v 3). Jesus is fully God. He is the "only Son" of God. He is as divine as the Father.

EXPLORE MORE

Read Heb 1 v 4-14. What does the writer say about the relationship of Jesus to the angels? Jesus is superior to the angels in ability and status for He is the unique Son of God, to whom all authority is given. The readers of Hebrews may have attached a lot of importance to angels, but chapter 1 says Jesus is much more important.

Read Heb 2 v 1-4. According to Jewish tradition, the Law of Moses was given by angels. What does the writer say about the law? What does the writer say about the message of Jesus? The Old Testament law, which came through angels, was a binding word from God. Its message was that every violation of God's law received its just punishment (v 2). The gospel message, which we have heard, came through the Son, who is superior to the angels. So we should take this word from God even more seriously. Its message is one of salvation (v 3) and it has been fully attested by God (v 4).

According to Heb 2 v 1, what do these truths about the identity of Jesus Christ mean for believers? How can we drift away from the truth? What is the result of drifting away? How can we stop ourselves drifting away? Christians must pay careful attention to the gospel message that we have heard, so that we don't drift away. Get people to share how "drifting away" can happen. The results of drifting away are that we will come to ignore the message of salvation, and so we shall not escape God's just punishment (v 2-3). We can stop drifting away by paying more careful attention—discuss with your group how they can do this.

3. In verses 6-8 the writer quotes from Psalm 8. According to the quotation, what was God's intention for humanity? "Mankind" in v 6 refers to "man" in the sense of "humanity". Only in v 9 does the writer start talking specifically about Jesus. Although humanity was lower in ability and power than the angels, God gave humanity the honour of ruling over creation. God put everything under humanity's authority. We were created to rule over and care for God's world on God's behalf. See Genesis 1 v 26-28. There is no need to correct people if they suggest that verses 6-8 are also about Jesus, but make sure people understand what these verses say about humanity. Q6 will deal with the question of how these verses are fulfilled in Jesus.

4. What is the reality of human rule over God's world? V 8b draws a stark contrast between God's intention and the present reality. Humanity's rule is corrupt and limited.

- **How do we see this in the world today?** For example: pollution is a sign of humanity's corrupt rule; when people are addicted to drugs or alcohol, they are being ruled by creation (in the form of hops, opium and so on), rather than ruling it; natural disasters like earthquakes are examples of humanity's limited rule—they happen because God cursed the earth in response to humanity's sin.

5. How will humanity's role in God's creation be restored? Look at verse 9.

- **Compare what Psalm 8 says about humanity, and what v 9 says about Jesus.** Jesus was made "a little lower than the angels", which is the way the psalm describes humanity (v 7). Both were also crowned with glory and honour—however, this is not now seen in humanity, but it is seen in Jesus, who is crowned with glory and honour because of His obedience to death.

OR

- **Compare Adam and Jesus.** The first man, Adam, did not rule the world as God intended. Jesus is a new Adam. He will reign over the world as God intended for humanity (see 1 Corinthians 15 v 20-28). God's intention for humanity was to crown us with glory and honour (v 7), but our reign over creation was corrupted by our disobedience. So Jesus takes the position intended for humanity on our behalf.

Notice the contrast between "we do not see" (v 8) and "But we see Jesus" (v 9). Chapter 1 said Jesus is superior to the angels. In becoming a human, He became lower than the angels to restore humanity's honoured position.

6. APPLY: How should this truth—that humanity's rule will be restored in Jesus—affect our attitude to the environment? We are to rule over creation and care for it. Ruling over creation does not mean we can exploit the earth. We are to rule as God rules over us—a rule of love, life, liberty and blessing. The earth is not ours.

It has been entrusted to us by God. We are responsible to Him for how we care for it. Hebrews 2 gives us hope for the environment. By contrast, environmental movements may achieve many good things, but they cannot save human nature, and so they can never save the planet. Jesus is the only one who restores humanity's corrupt and limited rule. So Jesus liberates creation from its bondage to decay (Rom 8 v 19-21).

7. APPLY: "We see Jesus ... now crowned with glory and honour" (v 9). This is not how the rest of the world sees Him yet. How do we "see" Jesus like this? Christians see Jesus with the eye of faith, in response to what we have learned about Him from God's word. (See John 20 v 29-31 for an example of the link between having faith and hearing God's word.) This will make a difference to how we live in this world in many ways: we submit to Jesus as our King and do what He wants because we know that He is reigning right now; we devote our lives to spreading His message, because we understand the peril of those who don't recognise Him as Lord and King; we persevere faithfully in the face of opposition or persecution because we know that Jesus is in charge, not our opponents; we spend time in prayer to Him because He is the Ruler of creation; etc.

8. What does the writer mean when he says God made Jesus perfect (= qualified) through what he suffered (v 10)? Jesus needed to be "of the same family". He needed to be able to call us "brothers and sisters" if he was going to bring many "sons and daughters" to glory. Jesus needed to become human to save us. He needed to experience the full human experience of suffering and death. In verse 9 we are told what Jesus suffered—He suffered death.

At this point you may want to summarise the two aspects of Jesus' nature that we have learned so far this session: Jesus always was and is fully God. He is God's only eternal Son, the heir of all things, Maker of the universe and the exact representation of the Father's being (Heb 1 v 2-3). But Jesus also became fully human and experienced suffering. We call this the "incarnation" (= God becoming human). Jesus became the human representative of His people. We are His family; He is our brother.

9. According to v 14-15, why did Jesus become human? Jesus became human so that He could die as the representative of humanity, to set us free and destroy the work of the devil.

10. How does Jesus set us free? You may want to ask the following questions to help people think this through:

- **What are we set free from?** The fear of death. The devil uses our fear of death to enslave us.
- **Why do people fear death?** Because death is unknown; also because death means judgment.
- **How does Jesus set us free from judgment (see v 17)?** By dying and rising again, Jesus showed that death is no longer the last word for God's children. Jesus died our death, taking our judgment on Himself (v 17). The word translated "make atonement" is "propitiation", which means "to turn aside God's wrath". Jesus took God's wrath against sin on Himself so that it would not fall on His people.

11. Write a summary of why Jesus became human, according to Hebrews 2. (Use your answers to questions in this session to help you.)

1. Jesus became human as the new Adam to restore humanity's rule over God's world.
2. He became human so that people could become part of God's family.
3. He became human to die as our representative. As a result He frees us from the fear of death and turns away God's judgment against our sin.
4. He became human to help us when we struggle with sin (see v 18).

EXPLORE MORE

Read Matthew 1 v 18-25 ... What reasons do people give for not believing in the virgin birth? What do these reasons reveal about the people who put them forward? People doubt the virgin birth because they have never heard of this happening outside of the Gospel accounts, and because it cannot be explained by medical science. This reveals that they doubt the reliability of the Bible and the ability of God to intervene in His world.

Compare Isaiah 7 v 14 and Matt 1 v 23. Why is it important that Christians believe that the virgin birth was a true historical event? Jesus could not simply appear as a man. He had to be born as a baby to be completely human and to experience fully our humanity. He also had to be born in the family line of King David, so He could be the promised son of David who would rule God's kingdom (see 2 Samuel 7 v 12-13). But why was He born of a virgin? Few other doctrines seem to hang on this fact and the New Testament does not make much of it. Jesus may have been born of a virgin so that He would not inherit Adam's sinfulness, but the Bible does not say this. One reason we affirm the virgin birth is that it happened! This is what the Bible teaches.

The virgin birth also shows that the birth of Jesus was the fulfilment of God's promises in the Old Testament (eg: Isaiah 7 v 14 and Matthew 1 v 23). If the virgin birth was not a true historical event, then God's promises in the Old Testament are not true either.

What important truth about God's involvement in His plan of salvation does the virgin birth demonstrate? God promised Abraham a people who would know God. But Sarah, Abraham's wife, was old and barren. By promising a vast family to a barren couple and then giving them a child, God demonstrated that He, and He alone, would fulfil His promises. Now, at the climax of the story, the promised Saviour is born of a virgin to demonstrate again that salvation depends on God's power and grace. But Jesus was from God in a unique way for He was the Son of God.

12. APPLY: When we struggle with sin, how does it help to know that Jesus was fully human? *Verses 14-17:* the devil is called the accuser because he uses our sin to make us doubt that we are truly saved. But Jesus, our representative, has dealt with our sin by dying in our place. He has set us free from fear. *Verse 18:* Jesus knows what it is like to be tempted and to suffer. So He can help us when we are tempted.

- **What should we do then, when we are being tempted (see Hebrews 4 v 14-16)?** Practical actions that we can take when we are tempted include: "preaching to ourselves" about our freedom in Jesus; reading what the Bible says about how Jesus has dealt with our sin; drawing near to God in prayer through our sympathetic High Priest.

5 Matthew 27 v 11-54

THE SACRIFICE OF JESUS CHRIST

THE BIG IDEA

Jesus died in our place to set us free from judgment and death.

SUMMARY

It is clear from Jesus' trial that He was innocent (v 23). Yet the innocent one was condemned, while the guilty one—Barabbas—went free (v 26). Matthew is not just recording what happened, but pointing to the significance of the death of Jesus. We, though we are guilty, can be set free from judgment and death through the death of Jesus.

The Romans mocked Jesus because He did not conform to their expectations of a king coming in glory at the head of a mighty army (v 27-37). But Jesus is the King who gave His life for His people and reigned from the cross in love.

The Jews mocked Jesus because He didn't conform to their expectations of a saviour, for He didn't even save Himself (v 38-44). But Jesus saves us because He refused to save Himself. He died in our place.

The Jews mocked Jesus because He didn't conform to their expectations of God, because He died in shame (v 40, 43). But Jesus is the Son of God who reveals God to us (v 54). We see how seriously God takes sin—it must be punished—and how much God loves us—He gave His own Son. The darkness that came over the land when Jesus was crucified symbolises God's judgment (v 45). Jesus took God's judgment against our sin on Himself in our place. He died forsaken by God (v 46). He experienced the hell we deserve. As a result:

- The curtain of the temple was torn (v 51). The curtain kept people from the holy presence of God. Now, the way is open.
- The dead were raised (v 52-53). Jesus has broken the power of death and the new age of God's rule has begun (even though it is not yet complete).

Key issues: the identity of Christ, salvation, atonement.

OPTIONAL EXTRA

It can be very helpful for Christians to know a brief summary of the Christian gospel, which they can tell or show to non-Christians in a matter of minutes. People in the group may be able to share summaries that they have used in the past. Or it may be more appropriate for you or an invited person to give a brief presentation.

GUIDANCE ON QUESTIONS

1. At the heart of Christianity is a brutal execution. How would you explain the death of Jesus, and why it is so central to the Christian faith? This is an opportunity to find out how well people in your group understand Jesus' sacrifice of atonement on the cross. Those with little understanding of the Christian faith may take the view that Jesus was a good man who meant well, but was finally caught out by His enemies. Many will believe that Jesus died for us because He loved humanity, but will be unable to explain the connection between His love and His death. For those who can explain the biblical teaching of the atonement, it might be more helpful to discuss ways in which we can clearly explain this to others (see optional extra above).

2. What did Pilate make of Jesus? He was amazed that Jesus didn't defend Himself (v 14). The charge against Jesus was that He was a king (v 11). This would have made Jesus a threat to Roman rule, but Pilate could find no evidence of any crime that Jesus had committed (v 23). Pilate's wife also confirmed the innocence of Jesus (v 19). Note the importance of the historical foundations of the Christian faith and its claims to be true. This is reflected in the way the Creed mentions Pontius Pilate—a man documented in secular history.

- **Explore the motives and guilt of everyone involved.** The Jewish leaders were envious (v 18). Pilate wanted the matter out of the way (v 24), but Pilate's claims of innocence are not credible. The crowd were manipulated (v 20) into condemning an innocent man (v 23). So everyone was guilty except Jesus. In fact, the condemnation of Jesus is on us all (v 25)—we have all started from the point of rejecting God in our lives.

3. Who was guilty and who was innocent? Who was condemned and who went free? Jesus was innocent (by Pilate's own admission—v 23); Barabbas was guilty. Jesus was condemned to death and Barabbas went free.

4. What does Matthew's account of the choice between Jesus and Barabbas show us about the significance of the cross? Matthew tells the story of the trial of Jesus to give us a picture of what happened at the cross. Jesus, the innocent One, was judged so that the guilty—including us if we have faith in Jesus—can go free. This is taught explicitly later in the NT—see 1 Peter 2 v 22-24 and 3 v 18.

5. What did the Romans make of the claim that Jesus is God's King? The Romans made a joke of Jesus' kingship with a crown of thorns and a satirical sign on the cross (v 28-31, 37).

- **What do you think they expected from a king?** For him to come in glory with a large army. Jesus didn't match this expectation.

6. What did the Jews make of the claim that Jesus is God's Saviour? The Jews insulted Jesus and abused Him because He refused to come down from the cross (v 39-42).

- **What do you think they expected from a saviour?** Someone who would defeat their enemies and liberate their land. They thought a true saviour would save himself and come down from the cross (v 40, 42). This is the kind of saviour they would believe in (v 42).

7. What did the Jews make of the claim that Jesus is God's Son? The Jews taunted Jesus and mocked His claim to be Son of God because He wouldn't come down from the cross, and neither did God rescue Him (v 40, 43).

- **What do you think they expected from someone who claimed to be the Son of God?** The Jews expected God to come in power and glory. They couldn't conceive of God enduring shame on the cross (v 40). Or they expected that the Son of God would be rescued by the Father (v 43).

8. APPLY: Jesus did not match people's expectations of a king or saviour. What kind of a King and Saviour is He, then? Jesus is the King who establishes God's kingdom, not through military power, but through His death in our place on the cross. The Roman soldiers conducted a sham "enthronement" for Jesus, not realising the cross *was* His throne. Jesus is the King who gave Himself for His people, setting them free by dying in their place. The Jews expected a king and saviour who would defeat their enemies (the Romans). But Jesus was defeated by His enemies, for His enemies (humanity). So He has defeated our true enemies—sin, judgment and death. The Jewish leaders thought Jesus would save by coming down from the cross (v 42). But He saved by staying on the cross. He saved by bearing God's judgment in our place.

- **How can Christians still have wrong expectations of Jesus?** Some churches tend to downplay the message of the cross in their teaching or songs or evangelism, and instead, focus only on Jesus' miracles or the resurrection. Similarly, Christians may give most of their attention to what they believe are the mighty works of God such as healing, casting out evil spirits, or experiencing supernatural phenomena. They may not think much about repentance, or salvation, or the Christian life of struggle and opposition. If people do not understand that the cross was actually the enthronement of Jesus, and if their lives do not reflect the centrality of the cross, it is likely that they have the same false expectations about the claims of Jesus as the Jews and Romans did.

9. What is the significance of the darkness in verse 45? (Compare Psalm 105 v 26-28.) The darkness was a sign of God's judgment. Psalm 105 v 28 recalls God's judgment against Egypt in sending the plague of darkness (see Ex 10 v 21-22)—a judgment for rebelling against God's words.

- **If the darkness represents judgment, on whom did the judgment fall?** At the cross, God's judgment against sin fell on Jesus.

10. So why was Jesus forsaken by God (v 46)? Verse 46 is a quote from Psalm 22 v 1 (which Matthew has already alluded to in verse 35—compare Psalm 22 v 18). In his suffering, the writer of the psalm feels abandoned by God. On the cross, Jesus experienced the full extent of human suffering and godforsakenness. But there is more to it than this. It's not just because God doesn't intervene as we think we need Him to that the world sometimes feels godforsaken—it's also because God is revealing His judgment against us (Romans 1 v 18). God forsakes us in judgment because we have rejected Him. And ultimately, we will be totally forsaken by Him. Physical death will mean the end of earthly life, but spiritual death will mean being without God for ever. On the cross, Jesus not only died physically—He was also forsaken by God as an act of judgment against sin. The Father poured out His anger against sin on His Son.

EXPLORE MORE

Read Hebrews 9 v 24-26. Where does Jesus "go" in these verses? Jesus entered heaven on our behalf, rather than hell. He presented Himself as a sacrifice before God.
How does He set His people free? By paying the penalty of the sin that condemns and enslaves us.
What does it mean to confess that Jesus "descended into hell" or "to the dead"? It may not be helpful to think of hell as a geographical location. To be in hell is to be separated from the light of God and the love of God, and therefore from all that is good

and true. On the cross, Jesus experienced this to the full. This is what it means to say Jesus "descended into hell" or "to the dead"—Jesus was forsaken by God. **Note:** The belief that Jesus entered hell between Good Friday and Easter Sunday (sometimes called "the harrowing of hell") is based on 1 Peter 3 v 18-20. But the events of 1 Peter 3 v 19 (Jesus preaching to the spirits in prison) did not take place at the time of the events of verse 18 (Jesus dying and rising), but at the time of the events of verse 20 (the time of Noah). In other words, Jesus preached through Noah to the people of Noah's day. But they disobeyed and, as a result, their spirits are now imprisoned.

11. What is the significance of the torn curtain (v 51)? (Compare Exodus 26 v 31-35.) The curtain in the temple separated the people from the Most Holy Place—the most sacred part of the temple and the symbol of God's presence. The curtain kept people away from the holy presence of God. The torn curtain means the way to God is now open. Anyone can come into His presence. Sinful people cannot come before a pure God without being consumed, but now Jesus has cleansed us from sin through His death. (See Heb 10 v 19-20.)

12. What is the significance of the open tombs (v 52-53)? By dying in our place, Jesus has conquered death. He died our death so that we might have eternal life. The open tombs were the proof that death had been defeated. It no longer had power over God's people. Although Christians die physically, they will enjoy life after death in God's new world—the tomb can no longer hold us (see John 11 v 25-26 and 1 Corinthians 15 v 22-23). The resurrection of the dead was also a sign that the new age had begun—that God's kingdom had been restored. We now live in "the last days" when God's kingdom has begun, even though it is not yet complete.

13. APPLY: We do not expect God to die in shame. But the cross reveals the true God to us (v 54). What does the cross show us about the character of God? Philosophies and religions think of "God" as a distant Creator or an impersonal force. The cross shows us that God gets involved in His world. It shows us how seriously God takes sin: God judged and abandoned Jesus because of our sin. The cross reveals to us the extent of God's love: God gave Himself for us on the cross—He endured hell for us. The cross also demonstrates how great and mysterious is God's sovereignty (Acts 4 v 27-28): God used the ultimate act of wickedness (the murder of God) to bring about the ultimate act of love (the salvation of His people).

14. APPLY: What kinds of things do people think will make their prayers more effective?

- **Do you think God is more likely to answer your prayers if you have spent the day evangelising and fasting, and have prayed for over an hour?**

- **What does make our prayers effective?** The open curtain (v 51). In other words, it is only through the death of Jesus that God welcomes us into His presence and hears our prayers. Christ is our mediator and we can add nothing to His mediation. See Hebrews 10 v 19-22.

6 1 Corinthians 15 v 1-34
THE REIGN OF JESUS CHRIST

THE BIG IDEA

Jesus Christ rose from the dead to give us eternal life and to restore God's reign over all things. This fact should decisively shape our lives.

SUMMARY

In 1 Corinthians 15 v 1-11, Paul summarises the gospel or good news. It is the most important news in the world. The gospel consists of facts: Christ died, was buried and rose again. The gospel also interprets these events by saying that Christ died "for our sins" and "according to the Scriptures". These events were the climax of God's eternal plan to deal with sin and judgment.

In his gospel summary, Paul focuses on the resurrection and the people who saw Jesus after He rose from the dead. This is because some people in Corinth doubted the resurrection (v 12). They probably thought of it as some kind of spiritual (but not physical) reality—perhaps the idea that it is possible to find hope in despair. These ideas are still prevalent in some churchgoers today. In response, Paul shows that the resurrection was physical, and that it was an historical fact attested by many eye-witnesses.

In verses 12-19, Paul explores what things would be like if Christ had not risen. Our preaching and faith would be useless and false (v 14-15). We would still be condemned because of our sin (v 17), for the resurrection is God's "Yes" to the sacrifice of Jesus. Believers who have already died would be lost (v 18). And the Christian life of denying ourselves to follow Christ (Mark 8 v 34-35) would be pitiful (v 19).

In verses 20-28, Paul says that Adam was the representative of humanity, so that through Adam death comes to all humans. In a parallel way, Christ is the representative of God's new humanity, so that through Christ life comes to all who belong to Christ through faith. Jesus has ascended to the Father's right hand and has been given all authority. He is now restoring God's reign over the world and defeating all rival powers (even death). Humanity was supposed to reign over creation under God's authority, but this reign became corrupt and limited when we rejected God's authority. Jesus is now restoring this reign.

In verses 29-34 Paul says people who do not believe in resurrection live for the pleasures of this life (v 32). But Christians believe in resurrection and so we should live sacrificial lives—we are living for the life to come. The resurrection gives purpose and meaning to our lives—our service for Christ is not in vain (see v 58). One of the aims of this session is to challenge those who say they believe in the resurrection to live a lifestyle consistent with that hope.

Note: V 29 seems to refer to proxy baptism, in which individuals were baptised on behalf of dead relatives. It may be that some people in Corinth were adopting this practice. Here Paul neither condemns nor approves of it—that is not his concern. Instead, he says it makes no sense if there is no resurrection of the body. Other Bible passages suggest that there is no hope after death for people who refuse to believe and repent in this life (Luke 16 v 26 and Hebrews 9 v 27).

Key issues: resurrection, ascension, kingdom of God, judgment, discipleship.

OPTIONAL EXTRA

Ask someone to prepare a five-minute talk for the group on how they would defend the belief that the resurrection of Jesus was a real event in history.

GUIDANCE ON QUESTIONS

1. Share your experiences of events that took over your whole life as you were preparing for them. Forthcoming events that dominate our lives might be things like exams, a wedding, a long journey or a house move.

2. V 1-8 are a summary of the gospel—the Christian message. Why does Paul say the gospel is the most important news in the world (v 1-3)? Encourage people to explore the significance of what Paul says about the gospel in verses 1-2. This is the news that has been passed on from one generation of Christians to another (v 1). The gospel is what we stand on (v 1)—it is the firm foundation for the Christian life, keeping us secure in the storms of life and guiding us in times of confusion. And the gospel is what saves us (v 2)—it is the only hope in the face of sin, judgment and death.

3. What is the message of the gospel? Jesus died, was buried, rose again and was seen by lots of people. In other words, the gospel is the story of Jesus and what He has done. The gospel also interprets these events. The next question explores this.

4. What does Paul say about the death of Jesus? Paul says Christ died "for our sins" and "according to the Scriptures".

- **What does it mean that Christ "died for our sins"?** Humanity has rejected God and one day God will hold us to account. The penalty of our rebellion is death. But Christ died "for our sins". The death of Christ was for our sins because the death of Christ was our death. He bore the judgment of God due to us, in place of us. Note that this is an opportunity for people to summarise what was learned in the previous session and to practise giving a succinct explanation of why the death of Jesus is central to the gospel.
- **What does it mean that Christ died "according to the Scriptures"?** The events of Jesus' life and death were part of God's plan and the fulfilment of His promise.

5. How does Paul emphasise the reality of Christ's resurrection? Most of the focus of Paul's summary of the gospel falls on the resurrection and the people who saw Jesus after He had risen (v 4-7). Paul shows that Jesus was really dead. He was not only dead, but He was also buried. And then Paul tells us that many people saw Jesus after He had risen again. The historical fact of the resurrection of Jesus was confirmed by eye-witnesses. It is likely that many of these eye-witnesses were still alive when Paul wrote this letter.

6. Why does Paul emphasise the resurrection in his gospel summary (v 12)? Paul emphasises the resurrection because some of his readers doubted it (v 12). They probably still used the language of resurrection, but thought of it as only a spiritual resurrection. They may have thought of it in a general sense, as meaning there can be hope out of despair.

7. What would things be like if Christ had not risen from the dead? Encourage people to think through all the different implications of Christ not being raised that Paul spells out in verses 12-19. If Christ did not rise from the dead, then our preaching and faith are useless (v 14). Paul would be a liar because the resurrection was central to his message (v 15). The New Testament points again and again to the resurrection of Jesus. If the Bible is mistaken about something so fundamental, how can we trust anything else that it tells us? If Christ did not rise, we would still be condemned because of our sin (v 17). The resurrection is God's "Yes" to the sacrifice of Jesus—it is God's promise that the cross defeated sin and death. But how can death be conquered if it still has the last word? Denying resurrection means denying salvation. If Christ did not rise, believers who have already died are lost (v 18). And if Christ did not rise, then the Christian life of denying ourselves to follow Christ (Mark 8 v 34-35) is pitiful (v 19). Sacrificial love and self-denial only make sense with the hope of glory to follow.

8. APPLY: There are many opinions today about what happens after death. How is the Christian answer to that question more credible and more thrilling than any alternative? The Christian answer to what happens after death—the bodily resurrection of God's people, who will then live with Him—is more credible than any other belief because Jesus Christ has already been raised from the dead. The one who spoke about resurrection (see John 11 v 25-26) has come back from death to live for ever, and is the only person ever to do so.

But the Christian belief in resurrection is also a more thrilling hope than any other. Spend some time discussing with your group the differences between the Christian hope and other ideas about what happens after death which they may have come across. Popular beliefs today include: after death you cease to exist; after death your life-force becomes absorbed into the cosmos (though your unique identity will be lost); after death your spirit goes on without your body in some peaceful form of existence (details are usually rather vague); after death you will be re-incarnated as a higher or lower life-form, depending on how you good you have been (but you will have no memory of your previous existence); and so on. Reincarnation in particular is an attractive belief for many today. It may be worth pointing out the differences between east and west, which probably reflect the stark contrast in standards of living that are generally available to people. In the west, reincarnation is generally welcomed because it offers further chances to enjoy life on earth, whereas in the east, reincarnation is seen to condemn people to repeated existences in a painful and harsh universe, from which most want to escape.

By contrast, Christians will be bodily resurrected to live for ever in the presence of God in His perfect new creation. Christians believe that people retain their unique identities after resurrection, and enjoy a physical existence. However, everything will be wonderfully transformed into the perfection that God has always intended. And this unique hope is available to all who have put their faith in Jesus Christ to be saved from their sins.

- **How should the truth of the resurrection affect our attitude to the difficulties we all face: sickness, ageing, disappointment, failure, etc?** Take one or two subjects appropriate to your group. Compare the attitudes of Christians who are looking forward to their resurrection with those of others. At this stage, the emphasis is on hope and comfort, rather than perseverance and sacrificial living, which are covered in Q12 and 13.

9. In what way are Adam and Christ similar? They are both representatives. All humanity was "in Adam" and God's new humanity is "in Christ". When we put our faith in Christ we become "in Christ"—He is now our representative, rather than Adam.

10. What are the differences between Adam and Christ? Death came through Adam to all those in Adam (ie: all humanity), whereas life comes through Christ to all those in Christ (ie: all God's new humanity, who have faith in Christ—true Christians). It was Adam's disobedience that brought death, while Christ's obedience brings life (Romans 5 v 15-19).
Note: Make sure that people correctly understand v 22—the important point to bring out is that Christ's resurrection means resurrection for all those who belong to Christ (v 23). He is the "firstfruits"—the first instalment of the harvest (v 20).

11. The Apostles' Creed says that Jesus "ascended into heaven" and "is seated at the right hand of the Father". What is the significance of this? Jesus now reigns from heaven. Being at someone's "right hand" was a sign of authority (we still speak of a person's "right-hand man"). Jesus has been given all authority by the Father (Matthew 28 v 18), and He is now bringing everything under that authority. In the Garden of Eden, humanity rejected God's reign. Now, throughout the world, there is "dominion, authority and power" (v 24) in opposition to God. But Jesus will defeat everything that opposes God (v 24-25)—even death (v 26)—so that God's reign is restored (v 27-28). Verse 27 quotes from Psalm 8 which, as we saw in Session Four, speaks of humanity's rule over, and care for the earth. Because humanity rejected God, our rule has become corrupt and limited. But Jesus is the new Adam (v 22), who is restoring humanity's proper rule over creation.

EXPLORE MORE
Read John 5 v 19-30. Who will judge humanity? God will appoint Jesus as the judge of humanity (v 22, 27). **On what basis will people be judged?** Their actions (v 29). But the key criterion is whether people have believed in Jesus (v 24). Our good works are a response to our faith in God, while our evil actions arise from our rejection of God. Now that God has sent His Son into the world, our response to God's Son becomes the touchstone of our response to God. **When will judgment take place?** On the day of resurrection (v 25, 28). See also John 12 v 47-48; Acts 17 v 31; Rom 2 v 16; 2 Cor 5 v 10; Heb 9 v 27-28; 10 v 26-31.
Imagine someone cuts in front of you while you are driving your car. How do you respond? How should this truth change our natural response?
Read Rom 12 v 14-21. How should we respond when we are wronged? We often wish God would immediately send down a thunderbolt on people who wrong us. When we are impatient with God's judgment, we take judgment into our own hands with judgmental thoughts and vengeful actions. The correct response to judgmental thoughts is to wait for God's judgment and repay evil with mercy (v 19-20). **What does our impatience for judgment reveal about us?** That we don't trust God to do what is right. It also

shows that we don't understand what God's judgment will mean for us. See Malachi 2 v 17 – 3 v 2, where the people want God to come in judgment immediately, but Malachi warns that no one can stand before God's coming judgment. See also Romans 2 v 1 and 14 v 9-13. **How can we avoid being judgmental?** By reminding ourselves that we will only escape judgment because Christ has taken that judgment in our place on the cross.

- **Why do you think God doesn't judge people now?** God delays His judgment to give people time to repent (Romans 2 v 4-5; 2 Peter 3 v 9).

12. APPLY: If Christ has not been raised and we will not be raised, what would be the logical way to live? To live for this life only. Life would have no ultimate meaning, so we should just live for pleasure.

- **What evidence is there that people live like this today?** "Let us eat and drink, for tomorrow we die" is the motto of our culture.

- **Since there is a resurrection, what is the logical way to live?** Paul is prepared to die daily—to live a life of sacrifice, service and hard work. And he is prepared to face death (in v 32 from wild beasts). Since there is resurrection, then we should live for the life to come, rather than for this life—for glory, and to struggle against sin (v 34).

- **How do different ways of life reflect different views about the future?** Get people to share from their own lives as non-Christians, or from the lives of people they know. For example: those who don't believe in any future judgment will live as they want to; those who believe you live on after death only through your children or your achievements may do anything to have children or earn success. Invite people to consider what message about the future is given by their lifestyle (see also getting personal). In 1 Peter 3 v 15, Peter says people will ask us about "the hope that we have". In other words, people will ask about our faith when our lives reflect what we believe about the future beyond death.

13. APPLY: In verse 10, Paul says God's grace in his life was not "in vain" (ESV). In verse 58, he uses the same phrase again when he says our labour is not "in vain". It means "empty" or "pointless". The resurrection gives our lives meaning and purpose. What is that purpose (v 10-11, 58)? Paul's life is not empty. Although he is the most unworthy apostle (for he once persecuted the church of God —v 9), God's grace has given his life meaning and purpose—to preach the gospel of salvation in Christ. His life has purpose because he preaches the gospel (v 10-11), the thing "of first importance" (v 3). Verse 58 is where Paul applies this great chapter on the resurrection. He tells Christians to keep going ("Let nothing move you") and keep working ("Always give yourselves fully to the work of the Lord"). Give yourself in the service of Christ; live life with purpose; do not live an empty life.

7 Romans 8 v 1-17
THE LIFE OF THE SPIRIT

THE BIG IDEA

The Holy Spirit is God in us, enabling us in the present to live as God's children and raising us to eternal life in the future to enjoy the inheritance of God's children.

SUMMARY

This session looks at the role of the Spirit in the life of a Christian in the following ways: making what Christ did on the cross effective in the lives of those who put their faith in Him; enabling us to escape the control of the sinful nature; empowering us to put to death sin, and instead, to live lives that please God; raising our bodies to eternal life in the future; making us sons of God with a glorious inheritance to look forward to, and enabling us to call God "Father".

Romans 7 has described how the law of God exposes our sin and pronounces the penalty of death. In Romans 8 v 2, Paul says we have been set free from the power of sin (= slavery) and the penalty of sin (=death). There is no condemnation for those in Christ (v 1) because, in Christ, God has condemned sin (v 3). The work of Christ in the past on the cross is applied to our lives in the present by the Spirit. The Puritan William Bridge described the Spirit as "Christ's executor." Just as the executor of a will carries out of the intentions of the one who has died, so the Spirit brings the blessings of Christ's life and death to His family—that is, Christians. Notice that Paul describes the Spirit as "the Spirit of God" and "the Spirit of Christ" (v 9). Having the Spirit in us is the same as having Christ in us (v 9-10). The Holy Spirit is God in us.

The Spirit sets us free from the power of sin. Before we became Christians, we were controlled by our flesh, or as the NIV84 translates it, "sinful natures" (v 5). We were trapped by our sin, hostile to God and heading for death (v 6-8). But when we became Christians, we received the Holy Spirit (v 9). The Spirit enables us to live as children of God. We are now free to live a life that pleases God. But the habits of our old sin-dominated life continue. This means the Christian life is a struggle between the life of the Spirit and the old life of our flesh. Contrary to what we might think, this struggle is a sign of life—it shows that someone has truly become a child of God and is now living the Christian life (v 12-13).

The Spirit sets us free from the penalty of sin. The penalty of sin is death—that is, physical death (our bodies decay and die) and spiritual death (we are separated from God). Christians continue to experience physical death (v 10). But in the present, the Spirit gives us spiritual life (v 10), and in the future, the Spirit will also raise our physical bodies to eternal life (v 11).

The Spirit enables us to live as the children of God. The Spirit helps us realise we are God's children and that we can talk to God as our Father in prayer (v 15-16). As God's children, we have an inheritance in the new creation (v 17).

Watch out for two common misconceptions about sin in the life of a Christian. Some have understood that there is now no condemnation for those in Christ, but fail to realise that being "in Christ" means they are under the "new management" of the Spirit, who leads them to struggle against sin in their lives and put it to death. Instead, they become complacent about sin. Others wrongly expect to be fully transformed when they become a Christian, not realising that it is just the beginning of a life of struggle against sin in this world. The fact that the struggle is ongoing means they begin to doubt whether they truly are children of God. This passage tackles both errors, challenging Christians to fight to the death against sin, and encouraging us to be sure of our adoption as sons of God, and certain of the resurrection of our bodies in the future.

Key issues: the Holy Spirit, sin, sanctification, resurrection, adoption.

OPTIONAL EXTRA

We have become children of God, but often we continue to act like slaves. We are under the new management of the Spirit, but often we continue the habits of the old management of sin. To illustrate this idea, use an extract from a film that shows someone suddenly elevated to a high position, who then struggles to act in line with their new status (like *King Ralph* or *The Princess Diaries*).

(If you did not use the optional extra in Session Four you could use it here, with a focus on what it means to bear the family resemblance as children of God.)

GUIDANCE ON QUESTIONS

1. How do people today answer the question: What's wrong with the world? Share some commonly suggested answers and discuss how near or far from the truth they are. Many people would accept that most of the problems of this world are due to the shortcomings of people—it is generally believed that "no one is perfect". However, this is still very far from the explanation of the Bible. For instance, personal failings are commonly blamed on poor upbringing, inadequate education or social inequality, but not seen as the result of each person's rebellion against God. Nor would people link the pains and difficulties of life in this world—natural disasters, sickness, death etc—with the way in which humanity disobeys God. Whereas the Bible teaches that God has placed the whole of creation in bondage to decay, in response to humanity's sin. In general, people don't regard themselves as "in slavery" to sin—great faith is still placed in the ability of education, science and technology, the arts, political ideas or economic growth to resolve the state of our world.

2. What was God's law powerless to do? Go through verses 1-4 verse by verse. Discuss what has been done or is now true for a Christian, and why. By implication, you will see what the law was unable to do. (See table at top of next page.)

The law was unable to set us free from the slavery of sin and the penalty of death ie: "the law of sin and death" (v 2). And so it was unable to remove our condemnation (v 1). It could state God's righteous requirements, but it could not help us meet them (v 4).

- **What must be done about past sin (v 3)?** Our sin must be condemned through a sin offering—things must be put right and justice must be done, through payment of the penalty of death. The righteous requirements of the law must be met—we must be enabled to live a righteous life, and so freed from our slavery to sin.

  Note: It is important that people understand that the righteous requirements of the law are not met

Verse	What is done for the Christian	How / Why?	What the law couldn't do
v 1-2	No condemnation for those in Christ	Through Christ Jesus, the Spirit sets us free from law of sin and death which condemns us	Couldn't set us free from condemnation / law of sin and death
v 3	God provided a sin offering	God sent His Son in likeness of sinful man to be a sin offering	Couldn't provide a sin offering adequate for condemnation of sin
v 4	Righteous requirements of law fully met in the Christian	By the Spirit	Couldn't help people to meet the righteous requirements of the law

through what Christians do, but through the fact that they live according to the Spirit (which means that Christ, the perfect one, lives in the Christian—v 9-10). See also Rom 3 v 21-22 and 1 Cor 1 v 27-31.

- **What, then, is the purpose of God's law?** The word "therefore" in 8 v 1 shows that these verses are linked to chapter 7. In chapter 7 Paul describes how God's law exposes our sin and pronounces the penalty of death (eg: Romans 7 v 7-9).

3. The "law of sin and death" is the principle that sin and death dominate the existence and destinies of every human born into this world. How have believers been set free from the law of sin and death? (In answering, you will probably be re-stating some of the things discussed in answer to Q2. However, there is value both in reviewing these fundamental truths, and in allowing people more than one opportunity to explain them.) What the law was powerless to do, God has now done through Jesus the Messiah. God sent "his own Son", who took on our human nature so that He could die in our place as our representative (v 3)—Christians are "in Christ" (v 1). He took the death penalty of sin that we deserve so that it no longer hangs over us.

Note: "The likeness of sinful flesh" means Jesus became fully human without being sinful. He did not become a sinful man because He did not sin. But He was like a sinful man because He fully shared our humanity.

Don't let your group discuss these things as a dry and abstract "theory of atonement". Take them back to the opening statement of v 1—there is no condemnation for Christians because, in Christ, God has already condemned sin and met the requirements of His law. Get them to imagine what it would like to live on death row, and suddenly be freed.

- **What part does the Spirit play?** The work of Christ on the cross is a historical event. But it is because of the Spirit that this past event can work in the lives of Christians today, freeing us from the law of sin and death. So Paul calls the gospel "the law of the Spirit who gives life" (v 2). The Spirit is "the Spirit of God" and "the Spirit of Christ" (v 9). He is God living in those who belong to Christ (v 10-11).

4. What are people like who are controlled by their "flesh" (or "sinful natures", NIV84) (v 5-8)?

- **Which part of us is particularly affected by the control of the flesh (v 5)?**
- **What is the destiny of people who think like this (v 6)?**
- **What does it mean for their relationship with God (v 7-8)?**

By "flesh", Paul does not mean our physical bodies or appetites. He means our corrupt humanness—the constant tendency in us towards sin and self. This control by sin and self affects people's thinking (v 5). It is deadly thinking that leads to eternal death (v 6). It is hostile to God (v 7). People controlled by sin and self do not submit to God (v 7), nor can they please Him (v 8).

5. What happens when we become Christians, according to verse 9? When we become Christians ("belong to Christ"), we receive the Spirit. The Spirit is God living within us. The Spirit sets us free from the control of the flesh. We are no longer dominated by our old tendency towards sin. Notice that becoming a Christian and receiving the Spirit take place at the same time and are part of the same thing. Paul says you cannot be a Christian if you do not have the Spirit.

This does not mean you must have a dramatic spiritual experience to be a Christian. It means you receive the Spirit when you believe in Jesus, because it is the Spirit who enables you to see Jesus as your King and Saviour. You may want to look at Ezekiel 36 v 25-27 to see how the Spirit is the fulfilment of God's promise to enable His people to keep His law.

6. How is the life of the Spirit different from the slavery of the flesh? Look again at verses 5-8 and contrast the two types of people.

People controlled by the sinful nature	People controlled by the Spirit
Thinking controlled by the flesh	Thinking controlled by the Spirit
Heading for eternal death	Heading for eternal life (v 6)
Hostile to God	At peace with God (v 6-7)

Those controlled by the flesh do not submit to God and cannot please Him (v 7-8). Paul does not spell out an explicit parallel to this, but the implication is that those controlled by the Spirit do submit to God and can please Him.

7. Look at v 10-11. Why does Paul call the Spirit "the Spirit who gives life" in v 2? "The law of the Spirit who gives life" sets us free from both the power of sin (slavery) and the penalty of sin (death) (v 2). V 5-9 have described how the Spirit sets us free from the power of sin. V 10-11 describe the Spirit's role in setting us free from the death penalty of sin. Our bodies continue to be mortal, but the Spirit gives life to our spirits. And, even though our bodies will die, the Spirit will raise us up at the end of history.

- **How does the Spirit give life in the present and in the future?** In the Bible, death is both physical (our bodies decay and die) and spiritual (we are separated from God). Christians still experience physical decay and eventually death. But in the present, the Spirit gives us spiritual life (v 10), and in the future, the Spirit will raise our physical bodies to eternal life (v 11).

8. What is Paul's warning in verses 12-14? We are under an obligation to live according to the Spirit. We have no obligation to the flesh for we are no longer under its management (v 9). We are now under the management of the Spirit. If we refuse to accept the management of the Spirit, then we are heading for death. Some people may think that to live "according to the Spirit" must mean that a person lives perfectly. If that is the case, only perfect people will be saved. But Paul is not saying that—in verse 13 he tells us that those who live by the Spirit put to death the misdeeds of the body. That means that our struggle with sin is actually the sign that we are under the Spirit's management. On the other hand, if you are not bothered about living according to the Spirit, then you will not have any struggle with sin—you will just do it!

9. APPLY: What does it mean for us to "put to death the misdeeds of the body" (v 13)? A radical determination not to sin. See Matthew 5 v 29-30.

- **Does this mean that Paul is against the physical body?** Paul is not against the physical body. He has just said that our physical bodies will be raised to glory by the Spirit (v 11). Rather, he is telling us to put to death all the wrong things we use our body for—wrong thoughts of the mind, wrong looks of the eyes, wrong actions of our hands, wrong words from our mouths and so on.
- **What does the image of "putting to death" tell us about the Christian's struggle against sin?** It is not an easy or light undertaking—it involves determination, exertion and pain. There can be no surrender or compromise. The experience is not a happy one—we may be shocked or exhausted by the ferocity of the battle. But it is achievable (see Q10).
- **What might this look like in everyday life?** Encourage people to share what this means in practice for them.

10. APPLY: From these verses, how could you encourage and challenge someone who says: "I can't help sinning"? Notice in v 13 that Paul tells us to do something—to "put to death the misdeeds of the body". This is not something that we just wait to happen to us; it involves determination and action on our part. But also notice that Paul tells us to do this "by the Spirit". When we do it, the Spirit helps us. Before we received the Spirit, our struggle against sin was impossible. But by the Spirit, we can now do what was once impossible—we can choose not to sin. Of course, sooner rather than later, we will again fall into another sin—but that can be a further opportunity to experience the power of the Spirit in destroying one more sin.

11. What does Paul say the Spirit does for Christians in v 14-17? Christians are led by the Spirit and those who are led by the Spirit are the children of God (v 14). The Spirit is the one who "brought about your adoption to sonship" (v 15, see also v 23). By the Spirit we call God "Father" (v 15). The Spirit testifies with our spirit that we are God's children
(v 16). Ask people what this means in practice or in their experience. Eg: it is the

Spirit who makes prayer more than talking to the ceiling.

12. Look again at verses 14-17. What does it mean to be children of God? Encourage people to answer this question by looking at verses 14-17. The children of God do not need to fear God (v 15). We are no longer slaves (v 15)—we no longer cringe in fear before our Master. Now we enjoy the freedom of children. We can know God as Father and talk to Him in prayer (v 16). And we are God's heirs (v 17)—we will receive an inheritance in the new creation.

EXPLORE MORE

What are the links [between how God brought His people from Egypt to the promised land, and what God has done for us through His Son and Spirit]? Christians are set free from the slavery of sin and the fear of death. We are led by the Spirit. Paul warns us not to go back to the old life when we were ruled by our sinful natures. We have become sons of God, calling Him "Abba, Father" through the Spirit. And Christians are heirs of glory. In Romans 4 v 13 Paul reminds his readers that God promised Abraham the land of Canaan—except that Paul actually says God made Abraham "heir of the world". Canaan was only the beginning—God's ultimate plan was a new humanity in a new creation (see Romans 8 v 19-21). Christians are now the children of Abraham (Romans 4 v 16). Alternative headings for the two columns in the table in Q6 could be "the children of Abraham by nature" and "the children of Abraham by faith".

13. Summarise what v 1-17 say about the role of the Holy Spirit in the life of the believer. The Spirit makes what Christ did on the cross real in our lives. He enables us to escape the control of the sinful nature. He gives us spiritual life and power now so that we put to death sin and, instead, live lives that please God. And in the future, He will raise our bodies to eternal life. The Spirit makes us God's sons with a glorious inheritance to look forward to. The Spirit enables us to call on God as our Father.

14. APPLY: Imagine someone who doubts they are a Christian because they continue to sin. What would you say to them? First, you might want to ensure that they had truly turned back to God (repented) and put their faith in Christ, since they may not have any assurance about being forgiven because they are not yet saved. They may still be controlled by their flesh, and so hostile to God (v 5-8). But if they have put their faith in Christ, then you could remind them that struggling with a sin is a sign of the Spirit at work in us (v 12-14). If they continue to pray, then you could remind them that prayer is a sign of the Spirit's work in us (v 15-16). Above all, you can remind them that there is no condemnation for those in Christ because our sin was condemned on the cross (v 1-3). And pray that the Spirit will testify to their spirits that they are God's children (v 16).

8 Ephesians 1 – 4
THE COMMUNITY OF THE SPIRIT

THE BIG IDEA
The church is at the centre of the Father's plan of salvation; it is the bride for whom Christ died; and it is the community in which the Holy Spirit lives.

SUMMARY
The letter of Ephesians is all about the privileges of being the church of Christ, and the responsibilities of living as the church. As you dip into Ephesians to learn more about what the church truly is, you should be praying that people in your group will never view church in the same way again.

The Apostles' Creed says we believe in "the holy catholic Church, the communion of saints." To be correctly understood, these terms will probably need to be explained to most people.

"Holy" does not mean the church now is without fault. It means our sins are forgiven (1 v 7). We have been cleansed by the gospel (5 v 26). And one day Christ will present us as His perfect, radiant bride (5 v 27; 1 v 4).

"Catholic" does not mean Roman Catholic. It means universal. The church is for everyone who believes, no matter what their ethnic or social background. By reconciling us to God, Christ has reconciled us to one another (2 v 11-18). Salvation and church membership are based entirely on what Christ has done so there can be nothing about us that marks us out as superior. We all have equal access to the Father through the Son by the Spirit (2 v 18).

"Communion" here does not mean the Lord's Supper or Eucharist. It means community or fellowship. We have been reconciled by Christ and so we should make every effort to be united (4 v 1-6). Churches are to be communities of love and care (4 v 25 – 5 v 2).

"Holy ones" is the way the NIV2011 translates "saints". All God's people are called saints (1 v 1). Everyone in the church has a role to play. Paul says all God's people serve God and build up the church—not just church leaders. The role of church leaders is to equip Christians for this work (4 v 7-13).

Key issues: the church, reconciliation, ministry, mission.

OPTIONAL EXTRA
The church is in a spiritual battle (6 v 10-12). It is a battle to proclaim the truth in a world full of Satan's lies (6 v 17). The church has a mission to tell others the gospel (6 v 19-20). Ask people to imagine they are a church-planting team in, say, Spain. How would they spend their time? How would they view their jobs? How would they make decisions? What opportunities would they be looking for? What would their meetings be like? At the end of the discussion, make the point that we are all missionaries in our current situations. We should adopt the same attitude where we are now as if we were missionaries in another country.

GUIDANCE ON QUESTIONS
1. "Jesus is okay; it's the church I can't stand." Why do people say things like this? How do you react to these kinds of statements? Answers to this question will throw up mainly negative views of church,

some of which the people in your group may share.

2. What does Paul these Christians (v 1). What is he telling them about the Christian life? "Holy Ones" (or "saints", NIV84). Paul is not talking about special super-Christians, but all the Christians in Ephesus. The Christian life is about being holy (disctinctive, or set apart). When the Apostles' Creed talks of "the saints", it is talking about all Christians.

3. From this passage, what does it mean to say the church is a holy community? (See also Eph 5 v 25-27.)

- 1 v 1-7: The church is the community of people who have had their sins forgiven (v 7). They were chosen by God to be holy (v 4). They are called "saints" ("holy ones"—v 1).
- 5 v 25-27: Paul says Jesus Christ died to make the church holy. He cleansed her and will present her as a radiant and holy bride.

- **How can the church be a holy community if Christians are not perfect?** God regards us as holy because our sins are forgiven. We are holy in God's sight because He sees us "in Christ". And one day we will truly be holy and blameless before Him. Notice that our holiness before God is not our achievement, but God's gracious work (v 6).

4. Summarise what God the Father has done for Christ. God has given all authority to Christ (v 20-22). See also 1 v 10 and 3 v 10-11. God's ultimate plan is to bring all things together under Christ (1 v 10).

- **What role does the church play in this plan?** "The rulers and authorities in the heavenly realms" in 3 v 10 are the spiritual forces of evil (see 6 v 12). Through Christ, God is going to restore the peace and harmony that was disrupted by Satan. The church makes God's plan known to these spiritual forces of evil (3 v 10-11). But what is it about the church that shows now what God is going to do in the future? This will be answered in Q10.

5. For what purpose has God done this? Look at v 22. Paul says Christ has been made head over everything "for the church". Christ has been given all authority to guide, protect and bless His people.

- **Over what is Christ the head?** Everything (v 22).
- **What is His body?** Only His people (v 23).
- **What does Christ fill?** Everything (v 23).
- **What is described as the fulness of Christ?** Only His people (v 23).

6. APPLY: How do you generally think and feel about church on, say, Sunday mornings? And what do you think shapes your attitude?

- **Summarise what we have learned about the great privilege of being part of the church.** The church is not simply a convenient group for Christians to support one another. It is at the centre of God's eternal plan. God promised to save a people who would be His people—made holy (1 v 4) and adopted into His family (1 v 5). "Christ loved the church and gave himself up for her" (5 v 25). One day the church will be Christ's perfect bride. Individuals are saved when they become part of God's redeemed people through faith in Jesus.

The aim of this question is to help Christians bridge the gap that often occurs between their day-to-day view of church, and the place that church has in the plans and the love of God. Allow people to share how they often feel about church, and help them to identify where these views have come from. For instance, some Christians can be very critical and negative about church—they may think that church is about making them feel good and so are likely to be disappointed when Christians fail to meet their unrealistic expectations. Others may, deep down, find church a bit cringy—perhaps influenced by our culture, which looks down on what it sees as reactionary fundamentalists, annoying do-gooders, weaklings and weirdos. Those who are deeply involved in church ministries often view church with a sense of weariness—it's all about hassle and responsibilities and rotas.

- **To what extent do these attitudes reflect (or fail to reflect) the fact that church is made up of sinners who have been graciously adopted as sons of God, to be the bride, the body and the fulness of Christ, God's chosen and supreme King?** Encourage people to think about attitudes for a Sunday morning that will better reflect God's view of His church. For instance, if God has forgiven our Christians brothers and sisters at such cost to Himself, nothing should stop us from forgiving them and bearing with their failings. If God has placed the church at the centre of His plans, nothing should be able to persuade us that church is irrelevant or embarrassing. If the church is to be the radiant and holy bride of Christ, nothing should be able to stop us from encouraging and preparing one another for our glorious future.

7. What was the position of the Gentiles (non-Jews) before the time of Jesus? Note that the word "Gentiles" (non-Jews) also means "nations". Look at verse 12. The Gentiles were left out of the Messiah's kingdom ("separate from Christ"—the word "Christ" means "Messiah"). They were not part of God's people ("excluded from citizenship in Israel"). And they had no share in God's promise to create a people who know God in a place of blessing ("foreigners to the covenants of the promise").
Note: For those who are troubled by this fact, it is worth pointing out that throughout Old Testament history, Gentile people did become part of God's people, but they had to do this by giving up their own culture and allying themselves with Israel. Famous examples include Rahab (Joshua 2 and 6 v 17-25), Ruth, and Naaman (2 Kings 5).

8. What is the status of non-Jews now who are "in Christ Jesus"? In Christ Jesus, the Gentiles or nations have been brought near (v 13)—near to the covenants of the promise, to hope and to God (v 12). Those from any nation who have faith in Christ are now part of the people of God (v 19). You may want to compare 2 v 12 with 3 v 6, where similar language is used but "separate ... excluded ... foreigners" has become "together ... together ... together".

9. How has Christ made the church for everyone? Look at what is said in the following verses:

- **v 12-13: What has the blood of Christ done?** Made it possible for people from all nations to become part of God's people, and to enjoy all the promises and blessings that previously were only for Israel.
- **v 16: Who has been reconciled to whom?** By reconciling people of all nations to God, Christ has reconciled us to one another.
- **v 14-15 (also v 11): What divided people previously? What has Christ now done?** The law (and especially circumcision—v 11) marked out the Jews as different and separate (v 14). It was a badge of their distinct identity. But now faith in Christ is the badge of identity for God's people. The old badge of the law, which divided people, is gone (v 15).
- **v 18: What is it that unites everyone who is in Christ?** Because salvation (and therefore membership of the church) is based entirely on what Christ has done, nothing we are or do can mark us out as different or superior. We are all equal members of Christ's church. We all have access to the Father through the Son by the Spirit.

10. When all types of people are reconciled in church, what does this show God's enemies (3 v 10-11)? The reconciliation of people in the church makes God's plan known to the spiritual forces of evil. God is going to put right what they have destroyed. We, the church, are the sign that their time is coming to an end.

11. Look at verses 19-22. Paul describes the church (God's people, not a building) as God's temple. What does this tell us about the church? In the Old Testament, the temple was the symbol of God's presence, and the place where people met with God. But now the church is the place where God is worshipped and known. Worshippers in the temple could come before God by offering sacrifices, whereas we now come before God through the sacrifice of Jesus. The church is the place on earth where God lives (v 22). Notice that the temple is not the building in which a church meets, but the people themselves. Similarly, the church is a group of people, not a building.

EXPLORE MORE

... Discuss how you would use these verses to rely to the following statements: "I'm going to give up going to church. I can't find anyone like me there." See v 16. The church is a collection of people with different characteristics and gifts of the Spirit, but who are united by being "in Christ". It may be that I can't find anyone like me in church because everyone else believes something different from the gospel. In fact, that group of people is not a church because they are not "in Christ", and so I am right to give up trying to join in. But if I am looking for a church where everyone is like me in terms of age, personality, class, ethnicity or educational background, I have not understood the New Testament definition of church.

"We've had a couple of Christian newcomers at church recently, but neither of them were the sort of people we're looking for." See v 21-22. We may think that what our church needs most is Christians who are young people, or married couples, or well-educated, affluent professionals, or creative types. We are unlikely to seek out those who are destitute, or illiterate, or those with severe health problems, or dysfunctional families. And yet, if people like this are "in Christ", Paul says we need them in our church, as much as a body needs a hand or a foot. God is the one who brings Christians into our church community and each of them will be indispensable parts of the body.

"I never say anything about my problems at church. Everyone there is so stable and well-adjusted. I don't know what they would think of me." See v 26. It is sad when people feel like this about church. Paul encourages us both to suffer and to rejoice together. We may think that no one else has problems, but if we keep silent and pretend everything is OK we will give the same false impression to others. Openness about our problems encourages other Christians, who realise they are not alone in their own struggles. It also gives them an opportunity to serve others practically and in prayer.

What keeps the body together? We are all in Christ (v 12-13). See also Ephesians 4 v 4-6.

12. APPLY: Since all kinds of people have been reconciled in Christ, how should Christians live, and what does that mean in practice? Christ died to make us one and so we should "make every effort to keep the unity of the Spirit" (v 3). What that involves in practice is spelt out in verse 2. Encourage people to think through the practical implications for you in your group. Are there any ethnic or social groups that get left out by your church community?

- **What stops Christians from living like this?** People won't make every effort to keep the unity of the Spirit if they are out to serve their own interests first of all. Those who want recognition and respect can't be humble. Those who are interested in efficiency or success rather than people tend not to be gentle or patient with others. Those who go to church to benefit themselves won't bear with those who let them down or rub them up the wrong way. Those who look to church to have a good time can't be bothered to make the extra effort that is involved in keeping unity with people who are very different to themselves.
- **What antidote is found in these verses?** The antidote is to see the church as one body and to give priority to those things that bind us together with other Christians—the Spirit, the Lord, our baptism into Christ, our faith, our hope and our heavenly Father.

13. APPLY: Who in the church is responsible for serving God and building up the church? Who is responsible for helping them? Look at verse 12. It is God's people who do works of service and build up the church. The role of leaders is to prepare God's people for these works of service. So everyone in the church is responsible for serving God and building up the church. The job of leaders is to help people do this. The list of leadership roles in verse 11 all involve God's word. Leaders prepare God's people for God's service through God's word.

- **How should this affect what we do when we meet together with other Christians?** Encourage people to give practical ideas of things that Christians might do differently in their meetings together as a result of understanding the two roles of leaders and members. For example, pray for the Bible teaching, be attentive during the Bible teaching and encourage the leader, and talk about the teaching with other Christians at the end of the meeting—particularly, how you can put it into practice. Pray and look out for one way in which you can serve someone else each time you go to church—thank someone for what they do, offer to pray for someone, offer practical help, spend time listening to someone, look after someone's children, talk to someone you don't normally spend time with etc. Make sure that everything you do will encourage others to join in and be more involved in the church community—sing enthusiastically, contribute during prayer times, and speak to newcomers or people on the fringe.

14. APPLY: What principles does Paul give for how we should live as members of the Christian community? It may be helpful to complete the following table: See table below. These verses are not written to individual Christians—they are written to a community of people. This will become clear as you highlight the reasons that Paul gives for the behaviour he commends. Encourage people to think through the practical implications for your particular group. People may like a time of silent prayer and reflection to go through their answers in the final column.

Verse	Right behaviour	Reason	Wrong behaviour
4 v 25	Tell each other the truth	All members of one body	Cover up or lie to each other
4 v 26	Sort out conflicts as quickly as possible	v 27: So the devil has no opportunity to create division in God's church	Nurse grudges, refuse to back down, reject or avoid reconciliation
4 v 28	Find honest work to do	v 28: So we can provide for one another	Earn money dishonestly, live off other people's money because we are too lazy or picky to get a job
4 v 29	Only say what builds up other people	v 29: To benefit those who listen	Unwholesome talk—grumbling, gossiping, cynicism
4 v 30	Do what pleases the Spirit	2 v 22: The church is where the Spirit lives—it is His community	Grieve the Spirit
4 v 31-32	Be kind, compassionate and forgiving	5 v 2: Because Christ loved and died for our Christian brothers and sisters	Bitterness, rage, anger, brawling, slander, malice

9 Matthew 9 v 1-13; Titus 3 v 3-8

THE WORK OF THE SPIRIT

THE BIG IDEA

God forgives our sins and gives us the Holy Spirit so we can live a new life.

SUMMARY

In Matthew 9 v 1-8, Jesus encounters a paralysed man. But instead of healing him, He forgives his sins. In doing this, Jesus shows that humanity's greatest need is to be forgiven and reconciled to God. He then demonstrates that He has authority to forgive by healing the paralysed man.

In Matthew 9 v 9-13, Jesus eats with tax collectors. Eating was a strong sign of acceptance in the culture of Jesus' day. Tax collectors were Jewish, but they were regarded as traitors to God because they worked with the Roman authorities, who were occupying God's land. By eating with tax collectors, Jesus was showing that God welcomes sinners—God's enemies, including us! And Jesus expects us to reflect the mercy we have received in the way we treat "sinners" and marginalised people.

In Matthew 15 v 17-20, Jesus says that our sinful actions come from the sinful desires of our hearts. We do unclean things because we have unclean hearts—not the other way round as the Pharisees taught. We are not sinners because we do sinful things. Rather, we do sinful things because we are sinners. Paul says the desires of our heart are sinful because we have "exchanged the truth about God for a lie, and worshipped and served created things rather than the Creator" (Romans 1 v 25). This means we cannot stop sinning just by trying to change our behaviour. In Colossians 2 v 20-23, Paul says legalistic regulations may look impressive, but "lack any value in restraining sensual indulgence". If there is to be lasting change in our lives, we need new hearts shaped by the truth about God.

In Titus 3 v 3-8, Paul describes how sin deceives and enslaves us. On our own, we cannot stop sinning even when we try. But God has given us the Holy Spirit. We had unclean hearts, but now the Spirit has washed us. We were born with humanity's bias towards sin, but now the Spirit gives us new birth into Christ's new humanity. We were enslaved by sin, but the Spirit gives us new power to live for God, free from sin.

Key issues: sin, forgiveness, justification, sanctification.

OPTIONAL EXTRA

You could begin this session by discussing what people think is the greatest need of your community, your nation and the world. A 2001 MORI poll found that people in the UK considered crime and transport to be the main problems in their local area. Another MORI poll showed that people thought crime was the main national problem and the environment was the main international problem. You could do your own poll. Compare these answers with the priority of Jesus in Matthew 9 v 1-8.

GUIDANCE ON QUESTIONS

1. What does our culture think about sin? You could explore what people think of a Christian view of sin—repressive, outdated. Many people think that the word "sin" only applies to sex. Discuss what behaviour is regarded as unacceptable in our culture—this is what people will think is sinful, even if they don't use the term "sin". The modern view of "sin" tends not to refer to any objective moral code (eg: the Ten Commandments). Behaviour which previous generations considered to be sinful because it broke a moral law or custom may now be thought quite acceptable, as long as everyone involved is happy with the situation. In other words, right and wrong have become relative—you can't clearly state whether a particular behaviour is sinful or not, because it depends on the specific situation and the people involved.

- **And what does our culture think about forgiveness?** People tend to believe that certain sins should never be forgiven (eg: paedophiles). On the other hand, they may also expect forgiveness for behaviour that is no longer considered unacceptable by most people (eg: ending a marriage), without taking notice of the hurt and damage that may have been caused. These popular views of forgiveness lack either grace or justice. Contrast God's forgiveness—see Romans 3 v 21-26.

2. Imagine what the paralysed man and his friends would have expected from Jesus, and compare Jesus' actions in verse 2. What does Jesus show us about God's priorities? People may be surprised by the way in which Jesus acts towards the paralysed man. Jesus is presented with a sick man, but He does not heal him! Instead, He forgives his sins. He heals him only to demonstrate that He has authority to forgive sin. For Jesus, having your sins forgiven is more important than being healed. See also Matt 18 v 6-9.

3. Look at verses 9-13. What do the actions of Jesus show us about God's forgiveness? Eating with people in the culture of Jesus' day was a strong way of showing you accepted and welcomed them. That is why the Pharisees find it shocking that Jesus eats with the tax collectors and "sinners" (v 11). Tax collectors collaborated with the Romans, who were occupying God's land, so they were seen as traitors to God. But Jesus accepts those who are God's enemies, showing that God welcomes His enemies.

4. How do the words of Jesus in this passage explain His actions?
Verse 6: Jesus says that His miracles demonstrate His authority to forgive sins.
Verses 12-13: Jesus says that, just as those who are ill need a doctor, so sinners need a Saviour. People who think they are righteous (though they are not truly right with God) do not think they need a saviour. Jesus quotes from Hosea 6 v 6. In Hosea's day, some people thought they were right with God because of their religious activity (their sacrifices). But God says that what He values is mercy that reflects His mercy. In other words, if the Pharisees were truly right with God, they would show mercy towards sinners instead of condemning them. They would mirror the mercy that God Himself shows towards sinners.

EXPLORE MORE
Read Hosea 1 v 2-3 and 3 v 1-5. How does Gomer treat Hosea? She is unfaithful to Hosea. She despises his love and commits adultery. She ends up an enslaved prostitute.
How does Hosea treat Gomer? He is told by God to marry Gomer, despite her adultery (1 v 2). And he is to continue loving her when she continues to be adulterous (3 v 1). Finally, he is to buy her freedom at his own expense (3 v 2).
What does their relationship teach us about God's relationship to His people?

Like Gomer, we have rejected God's love. We have committed adultery by turning to other gods. This was true of Israel, but it is true of all of us as well. But God continues to love us and ultimately He buys our freedom at the cost of His own Son. Encourage people to imagine how they would feel in Hosea's position.

5. APPLY: How should the actions and words of Jesus shape our view of ourselves? The truth of God's forgiveness should both humble and exalt us. It shows us that we are not righteous in ourselves. We are sinners. We are God's enemies. There is no place for pride. But the truth of God's forgiveness shows us that we are loved and accepted by God. He sent His own Son to die in our place.

- **How is this different from the attitudes of our culture?** By contrast, our culture minimises the problem of sin—for instance, we shouldn't be too down on ourselves; we can deal with guilt through positive thinking; the only forgiveness we need to seek is from ourselves. Sin is unimportant and forgiveness is irrelevant.

6. APPLY: How should the actions and words of Jesus shape our view of those who are "outcasts" in our society? Jesus spent His time with the rejects and outcasts of His day—even though the religious people criticised Him for it. He welcomed them, and they wanted to be with Him.

- **How is this different from the attitudes of our culture?** By contrast, our culture tends to believe that outcasts get what they deserve, and forgiveness in this situation is wrong, or at least misguided.

- **Who are the outcasts in your community?**
- **How could you demonstrate God's welcome to them?**
- **Who might criticise you for this?**

7. What is the source of our sinful actions? Our hearts. Our actions do not make us unclean—rather, it is the other way round. The sinful passions of our hearts lead to our sinful actions. We are not sinners because we do sinful things—we do sinful things because we are sinners. The fundamental problem is humanity's rejection of God. Colossians 2 v 20-23 makes this point well.

- **How would you define sin?** It's not just wrong behaviour, but wrong thoughts, motives and attitudes (Matthew 5 v 21-22; 23 v 25). It's not just the wrong we do but the right things that we don't do (Luke 11 v 42). It's not just doing what we know is wrong—it's also doing what we think is right, rather than what God has said is right (eg: 1 Samuel 15 v 17-23). It's not just behaviour that harms other people—it's rebellion against God, our Creator and Ruler (Romans 1 v 18-21).

8. What happens if we just try to change our actions? If we try to stop doing bad things, we may have some success, but it will always be limited and short-lived (Col 2 v 20-23), because it will never sort out the fundamental uncleanness of our hearts. The Pharisees were wrong to think that religious activities, like ceremonial washing, could make them clean.

- **Read Ezekiel 36 v 25-27. What do we need?** A new heart, and that is what God has promised.

9. What does Paul mean in verse 3 when he says we were "enslaved by all kinds of passions"? Encourage people to think of how sin enslaves people. This is more than the slavery of addictions like drug abuse and alcoholism. If we try to stop sinning, we find we cannot. For example, we may try to stop being angry. But at best, we still feel angry in our hearts and at worst, our anger seeps out in one way or another. We are controlled by the sinful desires and passions of our hearts (see Romans 1 v 24-25). You may want to make links to Q8: we can't simply change our actions because we are enslaved by sin.

10. What are some of the ways in which we are deceived by sin (v 3)? We find ways of pretending sinful actions are not sinful—we think sin is not too bad; we blame others; we say we had no choice. Encourage people to give examples of the ways we are deceived by sin.

11. In verse 3, Paul describes what we were "at one time". What has happened to Christians to change this? God has saved us because of His mercy. And Paul describes God's salvation as "the washing of rebirth and renewal by the Holy Spirit" (v 5). We have been forgiven and justified (v 7). Paul focuses on the way the Spirit sets us free from the deception and slavery of sin described in verse 3.

- **How is this salvation an answer to the problems described in verse 3?** Now that we are justified, the Spirit lives in us and begins the process of setting us free from sin and helping us become more like Jesus (see Session 7). Note that the theological term for what the Spirit does in the life of a Christian is "sanctification".

12. Paul says that Christians have been washed, reborn and renewed by the Holy Spirit. How do these three things overcome the problem of sin? This question takes the three terms used of the Spirit's work in Titus 3 v 5 and links them with three powerful New Testament descriptions of sin. This will show the extent of the Spirit's work in overcoming the problem of sin in the life of each Christian.

- **Washed (see also Matt 15 v 18-20):** We do sinful things because we have unclean hearts. But now the Spirit has washed us.
- **Reborn (see also Rom 5 v 12):** We sin because we have inherited humanity's bias towards sin. We were born into sinful humanity. But now we have been re-born into Christ's new humanity.
- **Renewed (see also Eph 2 v 1):** Once we were dead in our sins (Eph 2 v 1) and enslaved by sin. But now we have been renewed. We have new life and power to live for God, free from sin. Highlight the fact that not only have we been "justified" (made right with God, v 7), so that all our past, present and future sins have been forgiven by God, but God is also changing us. He has given us the Holy Spirit to help us live a new life, free from sin.

- **Titus 3 v 3 says four things about us: we were "foolish, disobedient, deceived and enslaved". How does the Holy Spirit change each of these?**

13. APPLY: Paul teaches that without the Holy Spirit, we could not change. But what does Paul expect believers to do as a result of this teaching (v 8)? To devote themselves to doing good. This means that you make it a priority and involves great effort and commitment.

- **There is a connection between the work of the Spirit in changing Christians, and the responsibility of Christians to change. In what ways do people get this wrong?** God is working in us to change us and we are to work to change. Without the Holy Spirit we could not change. But we still have a responsibility to live a new life. People get this wrong in two ways. Either they struggle to change themselves without understanding or praying for the work of the Spirit in their lives (ie: without trusting in Christ for forgiveness of their sins). Or they wait for the Holy Spirit to take them over and transform their behaviour and lifestyle for them, without investing any effort themselves in doing good. The sign that a person is being transformed by the Holy Spirit is that they expend great effort in doing good and make it a priority.

14. APPLY: Paul reminds us in verse 7 that we are made right with God by His grace. But we still do wrong things. Being changed by the Holy Spirit is a process. What happens if we forget it is a process? In verse 5, Paul said we are not saved by the "righteous" things we have done. It is the same root word as "justified" in verse 7. Our salvation does not depend on the process of change. If we think change happens all at once, we might doubt we are truly Christians when we go on sinning. But we are not saved by what we do, but by God's grace alone. If we forget being changed by the Spirit is a process, we might think that Christians can be perfect in this life. See 1 John 1 v 8. Or, at the other extreme, we might think we are stuck where we are, unable to make any more progress in the Christian life.

---

10 Romans 8 v 18-39

THE HOPE OF THE SPIRIT

THE BIG IDEA

Christians can look forward with confidence to a wonderful new life in a renewed creation.

SUMMARY

Heaven is not a disembodied state somewhere on the clouds. The Creed affirms Christian belief in the resurrection of the body. This session aims to outline a truly biblical understanding of eternity, to encourage confident Christian hope, and to challenge Christians to live lives in this world that are shaped by future resurrection and eternal glory.

In Romans 8 v 18-22, Paul says the created world was affected by the fall of humanity. Humanity was supposed to rule over and care for God's world under God's rule. The created world now experiences frustration and decay because we rejected God's rule. But our redemption will mean the redemption of creation. In Christ, God's new humanity will once again rule over God's world. Christians look forward to a renewed earth.

In verses 23-27, Paul says we are waiting for the redemption of our bodies. The Spirit will raise our bodies from the dead (v 11) to live for ever in the renewed creation.

In the meantime, the Spirit is a firstfruit (v 23), or foretaste, of what is to come. Paul stresses that we do not yet have our final redemption (v 23-25). Health, prosperity and justice are not necessarily what we will experience in this world. Instead, the Spirit helps us in our weakness (v 26-27) as we "hope" and "wait" for glory (v 25).

Future resurrection and everlasting life are certain. Christian hope is more than optimism. It is a confident and sure expectation. Paul is prepared to endure hardship and death because of his hope for the future (v 17-18, 35-36). God's plan is to make us like Jesus and bring us to glory (v 28-30) and God's plan is certain. He sometimes uses suffering to achieve this goal (v 28—God works "in all things"). Our sin cannot disqualify us from heaven because the one who could rightly condemn us is the One who declares us righteous through the death of Jesus (v 31-34). Paul ends by confidently telling us that nothing can separate us from God's love (v 35-39). He says we can be confident because God loved us (past tense)—God demonstrated His love for us at the cross and nothing can alter this great fact.

Key issues: the new creation, resurrection, hope, suffering.

OPTIONAL EXTRA

Read extracts from the last three chapters of *The Last Battle* by C. S. Lewis. Lewis is describing events in his imaginary world of Narnia, but they are an inspiring, imaginative picture of the end of history and the beginning of God's new world.

GUIDANCE ON QUESTIONS

1. What do you imagine heaven or eternal life will be like? You may be surprised by some of the views of eternity that even Christians have. Some are not sure that resurrection means that we will have new, perfect bodies—they don't think that we will be able to recognise each other, or even ourselves! (This issue may have been addressed in Session Six.) Some who know the New Testament book of Revelation may take the symbolic representations of God's people in eternity as literal descriptions of heaven, rather than visual pointers to indescribable glory and perfection. People may think of being in the distant realm of heaven, far away from the physical universe that we know as home. They may fail to understand the truth that God is going to make a new perfect universe—that there will be continuity with the first creation, but that the new creation will immeasurably surpass the old one. Many get bogged down in questions of what will and won't be true of eternal life, and in the process miss the thrill of the awesome Christian hope. Watch out for these kinds of misconceptions as people in your group share their answers. This session aims to correct these kinds of misconceptions.

2. What has happened to the created world as a result of humanity's rejection of God? It experiences frustration (v 20) and decay (v 21) as a result of humanity's rebellion against God. In Genesis 3 v 17-19, the ground was cursed because of Adam's sin. As a result, there are now natural disasters, famines, suffering and decay in the created world. You may want to link this back to Hebrews 2 v 5-9 (see Session Four, Q3-5)—humanity has not ruled over and cared for God's world in the way God intended.

3. What will happen to the created world as a result of God's new humanity? Creation will be liberated from

God's curse and humanity's corrupt rule. Paul links this to the revelation of God's new humanity (v 19 and 21). Humanity in Adam was supposed to rule over God's world, but our rule became corrupt when we rejected God's rule. God's new humanity in Christ will rule the world as God intended, bringing freedom and life.

4. What are Christians waiting for? (See also v 11.) For our adoption as sons and the redemption of our bodies (v 23). Christians will die physically, but the Spirit will resurrect our bodies, just as He raised Christ from the dead (v 11). Our future resurrection is based on Christ's resurrection. Notice that, although we have already been adopted (v 15-16), we have not yet experienced this in full. A helpful illustration may be that of an adoption in which the court procedure and paperwork have all been completed but the child has not yet moved in with their adoptive family.

5. What do we learn about the life of eternity from verses 18-27? People often refer to eternal life as "heaven", and think of angels floating on clouds. But creation will not be replaced with heaven. "Creation itself will be liberated from its bondage to decay" (v 21). There will be a new heaven and a new earth. In Revelation 21 v 1-5, the new Jerusalem (the bride of the Lamb ie: the people of God—v 9-10) comes down from heaven to earth and God makes everything new. Sin will be destroyed (see 2 Peter 3 v 10-13), but creation will be renewed. And Christians will have bodies. Like Jesus, we will have resurrected bodies that are both remarkably different from our current bodies and yet also recognisably the same. The Creed affirms our belief in "the resurrection of the body", not the immortality of the soul only (see 1 Corinthians 15 v 35-57).

6. What does Paul mean when he says Christians have "the firstfruits of the Spirit" (v 23)? The Spirit gives us a foretaste of eternity. If your group needs help in answering this question, direct them to verses in Romans 8 that tell us what the Spirit does for Christians. For example, one day we will be adopted as sons of God (v 23), but already the Spirit enables us to call God "Abba, Father" (v 14-16). The Spirit enables us to experience the love, life, freedom and fellowship of heaven in the present (v 10). (See also 2 Corinthians 5 v 5 and Ephesians 1 v 13-14.)

7. How does the Spirit help us as we wait for our final redemption? There are a number of possible ways this question could be answered, but make sure people look at verses 26-27. Our weakness means that we do not know how to pray, but the Spirit, who knows God's will, intercedes for us. We don't need to worry that we will pray for, and get, the wrong thing. (You could also recap what we saw in Session Seven from Romans 8 v 1-17.)

- **In what ways are we weak?** Our bodies are dying (v 10); we struggle with sin (v 13); we are suffering at present (v 18).
- **What is the will of God (v 28-30)?** To make us like Jesus (v 29). (See Q10.)
- **In what way do we "not know what we ought to pray for"?** In specific situations that we encounter, because of our struggles with sin, the effects of ageing and sickness, and our weakness in suffering, often we do not know what God should be doing to make us more like Jesus. For instance, if someone is sick, should we pray for healing, miraculous or otherwise, or for strength to endure, or

for death? Some may agonise so much over this question that they don't pray at all. But we can be confident that the Spirit will take even our "rubbish" prayers and convert them into intercessions for us in line with God's will.

8. APPLY: God is going to give Christians renewed physical bodies in a renewed physical world (v 21, 23). How should this affect our attitude to our bodies and the physical world now? We should not despise or neglect our bodies and the environment. They are important to God—so important that Christ died to make them new. But it also means that what will happen to us in the life to come is more important than what happens to us in this life. See Matthew 10 v 28, 39 and 18 v 8-9. Encourage your group to think about the practical difference that this Christian hope makes to difficulties that we experience with our bodies, such as: ageing, disability, feeling ashamed of how we look, ill-health, and lack of skills or abilities.

9. APPLY: In verses 24-25, Paul says we are waiting for our redemption. What happens if you think you will receive complete health, justice or prosperity in this life, rather than in the life to come? Some Christians believe that all our problems (sickness, poverty and so on) can be solved now if we have enough faith. Others believe that God will liberate us from injustice in this world. But Paul says Christian hope is not true hope if we already have these things (v 24). If we expect prosperity and justice in the present, we will doubt God's faithfulness when we experience sickness or poverty. Or we will fall into the error of believing that God's blessing must be earned by our faith, and risk losing the peace and confidence that comes only from the true gospel of God's grace.

10. What is God's plan for Christians? See verses 28-30. God's plan is nothing less than that we might become like Jesus and share His glory. Encourage your group to grasp the enormity of God's plan—it's not just about personal progress or a better lifestyle or being a nicer person. Rather, the future for every Christian is the ultimate and most glorious perfection that can exist.

11. Why can Christians be confident about the future?

- **v 23:** We have received the Spirit as a foretaste of the future.
- **v 28-30:** God is working out His plan to bring us to glory. Everything that happens is part of this plan.
- **v 31-34:** Our sin cannot disqualify us from heaven because the only one who could rightly condemn us is the One who declares us righteous through the death of Jesus.
- **v 35-39:** nothing can separate us from God's love.

EXPLORE MORE

List the main questions that Paul asks in Romans 8 v 31-39. How does he answer each question?

- *Who can be against us (v 31)?* No one can be against us if God is on our side. And He has proved that He is on our side by giving us His Son (v 32).
- *Who can bring any charge against us (v 33)?* The only person who could bring a charge against us is God, and He is the One who declares us righteous (v 33).
- *Who could condemn us (v 34)?* The only person who could is Jesus, and He has died for us and intercedes for us (v 34).

- *Who can separate us from God's love (v 35)?* God loved us (notice the past tense in v 37) when He gave His Son for us, and absolutely nothing can change this fact.

12. APPLY: What difference should our future resurrection to everlasting life in glory make to the way we live now? Look at v 17-18 and 35-36. Paul is prepared to face hardship and death because he knows that one day he will enjoy God's glory. Use the follow-up questions to make people in your group think about the difference in their own lives.

What difference does the Christian hope of future resurrection make...

- **to your priorities in this life?**
- **to the likelihood that you will have to give up many good and enjoyable things to serve Christ?**
- **to ridicule and criticism of your faith by the world?**
- **to the possibility of persecution and suffering for Christ?**

13. APPLY: Look back over the whole passage. How should these verses help Christians who are suffering? *Verse 18:* We cannot compare our present sufferings with our future glory. Notice that groaning is a normal part of Christian experience in this life. Creation groans (v 22), we groan (v 23) and even God Himself groans (v 26), as we wait for final redemption. But groaning isn't so much an expression of despair or pain, as of hope—we groan inwardly as we wait eagerly for our bodily resurrection to glory (v 23).

Verses 26-27: The Spirit helps us pray when we are weak.

Verses 28-29: God uses suffering to make us like Jesus and this is our greatest good.

Verse 30: Nothing can prevent God's plan to glorify us.

Verses 37-39: Suffering cannot separate us from God's love, for God has decisively proved His love for us at the cross. At this point, it may be useful for people to share how they have been helped by these truths, or have been enabled to help others, in times of suffering.

CONCLUSION

Discuss with the group how these studies have changed the way they think about saying the Apostles' Creed in church. Do they think that they can say it with more conviction? Or are there areas where individuals need more study and thinking time to understand? What have been the most important things that have come out of the series for people?

You might end this final study by saying the Creed together (see page 6).

Good Book Guides

The full range

OLD TESTAMENT

Exodus: 8 Studies
Tim Chester
ISBN: 9781784980269

Judges: 6 Studies
Timothy Keller
ISBN: 9781908762887

Ruth: 7 Studies
Tony Merida
ISBN: 9781784983888

David: 6 Studies
Nathan Buttery
ISBN: 9781904889984

1 Samuel: 6 Studies
Tim Chester
ISBN: 9781909919594

2 Samuel: 6 Studies
Tim Chester
ISBN: 9781784982195

1 Kings 1–11: 8 Studies
James Hughes
ISBN: 9781907377976

Elijah: 5 Studies
Liam Goligher
ISBN: 9781909559240

Esther: 7 Studies
Jane McNabb
ISBN: 9781908317926

Psalms: 6 Studies
Tim Chester
ISBN: 9781904889960

Ezekiel: 6 Studies
Tim Chester
ISBN: 9781904889274

Daniel: 7 Studies
David Helm
ISBN: 9781910307328

Hosea: 8 Studies
Dan Wells
ISBN: 9781905564255

Jonah: 6 Studies
Stephen Witmer
ISBN: 9781907377433

Micah: 6 Studies
Stephen Um
ISBN: 9781909559738

Zechariah: 6 Studies
Tim Chester
ISBN: 9781904889267

NEW TESTAMENT

Mark 1–8: 10 Studies
Tim Chester
ISBN: 9781904889281

Mark 9–16: 7 Studies
Tim Chester
ISBN: 9781904889519

Luke 1–12: 7 Studies
Mike McKinley
ISBN: 9781784980160

Luke 12–24: 8 Studies
Mike McKinley
ISBN: 9781784981174

John: 7 Studies
Tim Chester
ISBN: 9781907377129

Acts 1-12: 8 Studies
R. Albert Mohler
ISBN: 9781910307007

Romans 1–7: 7 Studies
Timothy Keller
ISBN: 9781908762924

Romans 8–16: 7 Studies
Timothy Keller
ISBN: 9781910307311

1 Corinthians 1–9:
7 Studies
Mark Dever
ISBN: 9781908317681

1 Corinthians 10–16:
8 Studies
Mark Dever & Carl Laferton
ISBN: 9781908317964

2 Corinthians 1–7:
9 Studies
James Hughes
ISBN: 9781906334758

Galatians: 7 Studies
Timothy Keller
ISBN: 9781908762559

Ephesians: 10 Studies
Thabiti Anyabwile
ISBN: 9781907377099

Ephesians: 8 Studies
Richard Coekin
ISBN: 9781910307694

Colossians: 6 Studies
Mark Meynell
ISBN: 9781906334246

1 Thessalonians:
7 Studies
Mark Wallace
ISBN: 9781904889533

2 Timothy: 7 Studies
Mark Mulryne
ISBN: 9781905564569

Titus: 5 Studies
Tim Chester
ISBN: 9781909919631

Hebrews: 8 Studies
Michael Kruger
ISBN: 9781984986049

James: 6 Studies
Sam Allberry
ISBN: 9781910307816

1 Peter: 5 Studies
Tim Chester
ISBN: 9781907377853

1 Peter: 6 Studies
Juan R. Sanchez
ISBN: 9781784980177

1 John: 7 Studies
Nathan Buttery
ISBN: 9781904889953

Revelation 2–3: 7 Studies
Jonathan Lamb
ISBN: 9781905564682

TOPICAL

Heaven: 6 Studies
Andy Telfer
ISBN: 9781909919457

Biblical Womanhood:
10 Studies
Sarah Collins
ISBN: 9781907377532

The Holy Spirit: 8 Studies
Pete & Anne Woodcock
ISBN: 9781905564217

Promises Kept: Bible Overview 9 Studies
Carl Laferton
ISBN: 9781908317933

Making Work Work:
8 Studies
Marcus Nodder
ISBN: 9781908762894

Women of Faith:
8 Studies
Mary Davis
ISBN: 9781904889526

Meeting Jesus: 8 Studies
Jenna Kavonic
ISBN: 9781905564460

Man of God: 10 Studies
Anthony Bewes & Sam Allberry
ISBN: 9781904889977

Contentment: 6 Studies
Anne Woodcock
ISBN: 9781905564668

The Apostles' Creed:
10 Studies
Tim Chester
ISBN: 9781905564415

Experiencing God:
6 Studies
Tim Chester
ISBN: 9781906334437

Real Prayer: 7 Studies
Anne Woodcock
ISBN: 9781910307595

The Five Solas: 6 Studies
Jason Helopoulos
ISBN: 9781784981501

BIBLICAL | RELEVANT | ACCESSIBLE

At The Good Book Company, we are dedicated to helping Christians and local churches grow. We believe that God's growth process always starts with hearing clearly what he has said to us through his timeless word—the Bible.

Ever since we opened our doors in 1991, we have been striving to produce Bible-based resources that bring glory to God. We have grown to become an international provider of user-friendly resources to the Christian community, with believers of all backgrounds and denominations using our books, Bible studies, devotionals, evangelistic resources, and DVD-based courses.

We want to equip ordinary Christians to live for Christ day by day, and churches to grow in their knowledge of God, their love for one another, and the effectiveness of their outreach.

Call us for a discussion of your needs or visit one of our local websites for more information on the resources and services we provide.

Your friends at The Good Book Company

thegoodbook.com | thegoodbook.co.uk
thegoodbook.com.au | thegoodbook.co.nz
thegoodbook.co.in